The Villages of Aberdeen
Footdee

In this refreshingly original and pains-
takingly researched history of Footdee, the first
major study of Aberdeen's famous fishing village, Diane Morgan examines the evolution of
the Fisher Squares, explores the lost hinterland
of Upper Fittie and recalls the shipyards of the
Duthies, Walter Hood, Alexander Hall and
Hall Russell whose vessels carried the fame of
Footdee and of Aberdeen throughout the world.

By the same author

'Villages of Aberdeen' series

Round About Mounthooly

The Spital

Front Cover
North Square, Footdee.
From the original watercolour by J.A.Sutherland

The Villages of Aberdeen

Footdee
and her Shipyards

Diane Morgan

Denburn Books
ABERDEEN

In Memory

of the
Laing, Scott and Ross Families
and the members of West St.Clement's
(St. Clement's UF) 1843 - 1987

First published 1993

Re-issued with Postscript, 1997

British Library Cataloguing in Publication Data
A catalogue record for this book is available from the British Library

ISBN 1 898645 01 9

Printed by Printagraph, The Print Factory, Aberdeen.

Acknowledgements

I would like to express my thanks to the Aberdeen City Archivist Judith Cripps for her encouragement and her advice on numerous aspects of the subjects, and for her permission to make a draft of feuing plans of the early shipyards; to the Grampian Regional Archivist, Brenda Cluer and staff; to Frank Donnelly who has given sterling support; to the staff of the Local Collection, Aberdeen City Libraries and to John Edwards, Keeper of Maritime History and Michael Dey, Assistant Keeper of Science, Technology and Industry, both of Aberdeen Art Gallery.

I am much indebted to the following for their time and assistance: George and Ruby Wesbter, John Gillanders, Thelma Cowper, Ethel Kilgour and Albert Elrick; to Ann Johnston for her advice on St Fotin; to former Hall Russell staff James Fraser, Jock Smith and John Souter for their invaluable comments; to the management of John Fleming & Co. Ltd., and Scotoil Services Ltd., to Ean Emslie, Messrs Stronachs, Ken Guyan and to everyone who kindly took the time to respond to my queries.

My warmest thanks go to Pat and Jimmy Sutherland, the designers of this book, without whose help and enthusiasm its production would not have been possible; and to my husband for patiently chauffering me around Fittie. There are more interesting things to do on a Sunday afternoon than drive along 'the wynd callit Garvockis Wynd at the north end of the toun of Futtie' - or what is left of it.

I am grateful to everyone who provided illustrations outwith the author's collection and have acknowledged them individually. The front cover and the illustrations on pages 3, 53, 70, 83, and 135 are by Jimmy Sutherland.

Diane Morgan, 1993

The re-issue of 1997 includes a postscript which outlines the major changes in the area since 1993. My thanks to John Gillanders for his invaluable assistance, and to Lt.-Com. Bob Wilson RN for advising on the fate of the Hall Russell's Peacock Class Patrol Vessels.

DM, 1997

Contents

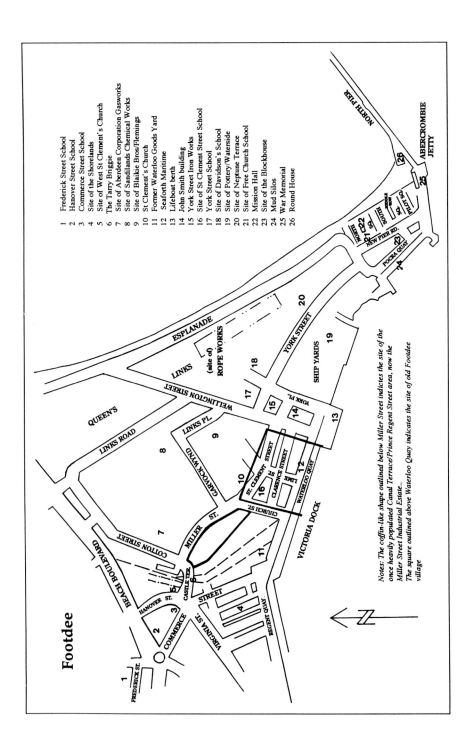

Footdee

1 Frederick Street School
2 Hanover Street School
3 Commerce Street School
4 Site of the Shorelands
5 Site of West St Clement's Church
6 The Tarry Briggie
7 Site of Aberdeen Corporation Gasworks
8 Site of Sandilands Chemical Works
9 Site of Blaikie Bros/Flemings
10 St Clement's Church
11 Former Waterloo Goods Yard
12 Seaforth Maritime
13 Lifeboat berth
14 John Smith building
15 York Street Iron Works
16 Site of St Clement Street School
17 York Street School
18 Site of Davidson's School
19 Site of Pottery/Waterside
20 Site of Neptune Terrace
21 Site of Free Church School
22 Mission Hall
23 Site of the Blockhouse
24 Mud Silos
25 War Memorial
26 Round House

Notes: The coffin-like shape outlined below Miller Street indictes the site of the
once heavily populated Canal Terrace/Prince Regent Street area, now the
Miller Street Industrial Estate...
The square outlined above Waterloo Quay indicates the site of old Footdee
village

Introduction

A small fishing village called Futtie, or Footdee as some of late affect to spell it from a mistaken etymology....

Aberdeen: Statistical Account of Scotland 1791-99

Ask an Aberdonian about Footdee, alias Fittie, and you're likely to be told that it is the old fishing village at the harbour mouth consisting of North, South and Pilot Squares and New Pier Road. This Footdee, however, is an official creation of the early nineteenth century. The original Footdee village evolved between Garvock Wynd and the former Hall Russell shipyard and bordered a beach of sand and gravel that is now Waterloo Quay. One sector, the Fish Toun relocated to its present site, then a bleak and remote area known as the Sandness, under rather curious circumstances in 1808.

Regarded as a village in its own right, Footdee has nevertheless always been within the Inner Marches of Aberdeen though termed a 'suburb' in earlier times. It gave its name to one of the four quarters of the city created during the fifteenth century for purposes of defence. In 1833 it became part of the First Ward, and fifty years later, under the Aberdeen Extension and Improvement Act, part of St Clement's Ward. At time of writing it is within the Castlehill Ward.

The name Footdee causes controversy. If rivers had feet as opposed to mouths and Footdee truly meant at the foot of the Dee, Torry on the opposite side of the harbour would have a greater claim to the name since the Dee flows seawards on the Torry side. But Footdee appears to derive from St Fotin, a second century martyr whose cult spread to the north of Scotland. A chapel was consecrated to him; perhaps near the site of the present St Clement's Kirk. (Curiously, in the Charter of 1495 that created Torry a burgh of barony, Fotin is named as patron saint, though a later saint, Fittick, seems to have proselytised there in person). St Fotin was subsequently ousted as patron of Footdee by St Clement, a somewhat masochistic choice for a fisher community given that he achieved martyrdom by being tied to an anchor and thrown into the Black Sea.

I have used the terms Footdee and Fittie interchangeably as Aberdonians tend to do, and have also used the older forms of the name as they occur in context, and hope not to have caused confusion thereby. Nowadays the term Footdee is spurned as a modern anglicisation of Fittie. However the earliest references, those closest in form to Fotin, are Fotyn, Futy or Foty. The fourteenth century de Foty family took their name from this area where they were 'prominent feuars'. In a Charter of 1601, the word appears as Fittie. Parson Gordon of Rothiemay the seventeenth century cartographer calls it Futtie or Futty, as did Daniel Mearns, the ward's councillor from 1876, and Lord Provost of Aberdeen from 1895-98. In G & W Paterson's Survey of Aberdeen of 1746 it is FuttDee. The earliest reference to Footdee that I have been able to track down was made by Gregory Sharpe in 1732. And Footdee it remained in the late eighteenth century maps of Aberdeen. *Pace* the *Statistical Account* quoted above, Footdee is as respectable and indeed a closer corruption of Fotin than Fittie.

Our concept of Footdee has shrunk. Last century the Squares were not thought important enough to merit mention as part of the area. One source stated that Footdee lay between Waterloo and Pocra Quays; another defined the boundary as from the railway to the Bannermill. The railway in question ran from Waterloo Quay parallel first to the lower section of Commerce Street then under the Tarry Briggie to run parallel to the west side of Cotton Street, while the Bannermill was at the beach end of Constitution Street, a wide swathe of territory. The Elrick brothers who lived in Cotton Street certainly regarded themselves as Fittie loons, 'though from the west end of Fittie', while my own family would talk of going down to Fittie when they were setting off for West St Clement's Church in the lee of Commerce Street School. It is only with the depopulation of Upper Fittie in the post war era, coupled with the fact that it is now fashionable to live in the Squares that we have come to regard that area alone as Fittie.

I have opted for the older and wider definition, keeping in mind too, that the original village was considerably nearer the Castlegate than the Squares are today. And so Part I relates to the evolution of the Squares, Part II to Salvation and Education while Part III recalls the now largely vanished industrial hinterland of Upper Fittie as well as the quays, once the commercial heart of Fittie. Part IV is written in tribute to the shipyards whose names were synonymous with Footdee, and which built vessels that in their day were among the finest in the world; the yards of the Duthies, Walter Hood, Alexander Hall and Hall Russell.

Part One

The Villages

Well, North Square, Footdee

3

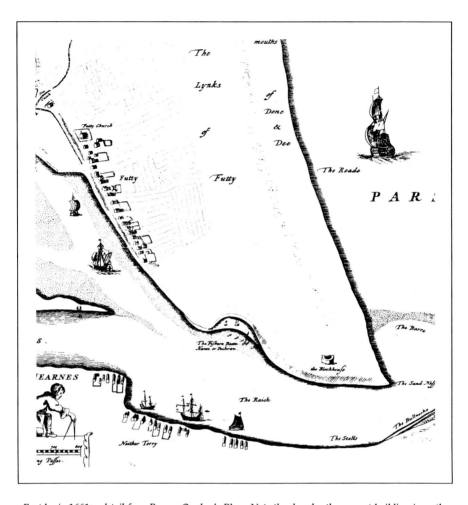

Footdee in 1661, a detail from Parson Gordon's Plan. Note the church - the present building is on the same site - and the rigs behind the cottages of the Fish Toun. 'The Fishers Boate Haven or Pockraw' latterly became the site of the Hall Russell shipyard. East of the Blockhouse is 'The Sandnesse', where the Fish Toun was relocated. Torry lies opposite.

Chapter 1

Futty Gate: the Highway to Footdee

The Castlehill, the Green Meadow, the suburb called Fittie, the
Haven, the Blockhouse, the Pier of Aberdeen...
from a Charter of James VI, August 14, 1601

The Futty Gate or highway to Footdee and its continuation the Road to
Pocra indicated in the Charter above, in modern terms the route by Castle
Terrace, Miller Street, St Clement Street and York Street to Pocra Quay - 'the
Pier of Aberdeen' - is an ancient one of great strategic importance. The
traveller would first pass through the Futty Port in the Castlegate, whose site
near the Salvation Army Citadel is nowadays indicated by a plaque. This
gateway, in use between the fifteenth and late eighteenth centuries, was built
as a defence against enemies seeking to attack the burgh after disembarking
at Footdee. In 1710 we learn that the gates were ordered to be repaired with
oak beams when a French invasion seemed imminent. It seems to have been
more frequently used however, for purposes of quarantine. In 1498, for
example, the magistrates ordained that 'the porte of the Castlegate passand to
Futy be closit' for the 'kepin of the toune fra the pestilence and strange seiknes'.
Immediately beyond the Port lay Futty Wynd which is clearly marked in
Parson James Gordon's invaluable Plan of 1661 which accompanied his
Description of Both Towns of Aberdeen. The Wynd predated the Port. Joseph
Robertson in *The Book of Bon Accord* (1839) identified a reference to it as early
as 1281, indicating a settlement of considerable antiquity at Footdee itself, a
theory that was reinforced by the discovery of a hoard in Clarence Street in
1867. This consisted mainly of coins of the English monarch Edward I, and
indeed the English army garrisoned Aberdeen in the late thirteenth century

5

Hangman's Brae, alias Castle Brae and previously Futty Wynd around 1850. It was absorbed a few years later by the present Castle Terrace. The house, left, with the sign depicting a gibbet may have been an inn. The Sick Children's Hospital, later Cocky Hunter's, was built on this site. The large building dominating the Brae is Castlehill Barracks.

6

during the Wars of Independence.

The Wynd was later known as Castle Brae, and more popularly, as Hangman's Brae thanks to Johnny Milne, the eponymous executioner who would come riding up it on his white pony when he had work to do in the Castlegate. Unfortunate wretches were hanged there, 'looking down Marischal Street'. Numerous tales of Johnny, a well known Upper Fittie inebriate survive. He was either a farm labourer or dyker from Corse in Aberdeenshire who in 1805 was convicted of stealing beehives and opted for the post of public hangman as opposed to a sentence of seven years transportation. The 'package' offered him was tempting; a fish out of every creel, a portion of meal from every sack, a peat from every load, even a free house in Canal Terrace which ran in those days from Virginia Street to Church Street while his pony had grazing around St Clement's Kirkyard. In 1834, however, the Town Council resolved that 'the office of Public Executioner be abolished and

Johnny Milne the hangman is shown in the foreground at the fish market in the Castlegate, selecting a fish from a creel, one of his 'perks'. Behind is the Tolbooth and New Inn, today the site of the Clydesdale Bank. Note the dress of the fishwives, one of whom, far left, is smoking a pipe, and the size of the creels. The Market Cross has since been moved some yards to the southeast. Detail from Seaton's View of Castle Street, 1806.

7

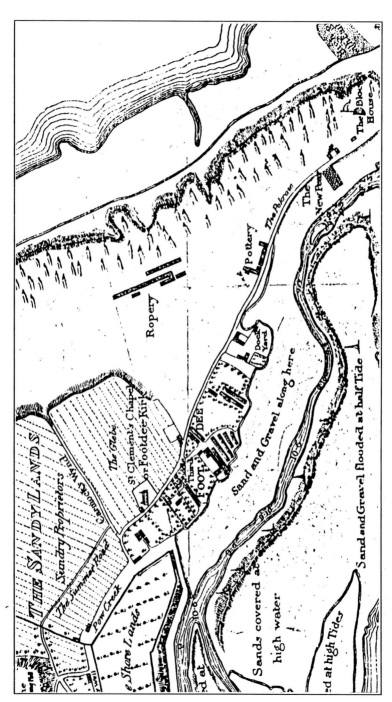

Taylor's Plan of 1773 shows the Summer Road top left, surrounded by fields, with the SandyLands stretching beyond. The Summer Road is truncated by Carnock's (Garvock)Wynd and the Road to Pocra (unnamed) carries the highway on to 'The New Pier (pier) built 1755, and the Blockhouse at Pocra. In the village, note the kirk and Middle Third, which in fact is a narrow passage. Fittie's first 'dockyard' (shipyard) has appeared as has the Ropery on the Links and the Pottery.

his residence in Canal Terrace be sold'.

Hangman's Brae, narrow, preciptious, enclosed by a dyke and paved with bluish causey stones vanished in the 1860s when the road was realigned. Castle Terrace - which some older Fittie folk even now refer to as Hangman's Brae - was superimposed over the original Brae and its continuation, Castle Lane. Today the steps running from Castle Terrace to the Virigina Street dual carriageway are roughly on the line of Hangman's Brae while the Lane has been completely absorbed.

Walking to Fittie by this ancient route must have been a pleasant experience. Looking across to the right while descending the Brae, one would have seen cornfields through which the Powcreek Burn flowed. The fields of the Shorelands beyond the burn had been reclaimed in the mid-seventeenth century when a new quay was constructed to relieve cramped conditions at the Town's Quay at Shore Brae. 'This key', Parson Gordon noted in his *Description of Both Touns of Aberdeen* 'runs downwards towards the villedge of Futtie no fewer than 500 walking passes, and it joyns with Futtie; a work of many yeires, oft tyme broken off' - thanks to the Covenanting Wars. The 'key' provided an alternative route to Fittie as its successors, Regent and Waterloo Quays still do. The reclaimed Shorelands did not stay long under crop however. By the latter half of the eighteenth century the Shoreland Improvements were underway to accommodate the increasing harbour trade and growing population. The cornfields disappeared under the warehouses and tenements of Virignia Street, James Street, Water Lane, Pork Lane (later replaced by Mearns Street) and the lower half of Commerce Street. An industrial scene greets one when descending Castle Terrace these days.

The Brae gave access to the Summer Road where again, fields stretched on either side. Nearest town was the Green Meadow mentioned in the Charter where folk who had byres in the Castlegate and Broadgate would graze their cattle, though as early as 1487, the Town Council had ordained that 'no catal sall haf pastour of gryss apone the lynkis', nearby but sacrosanct. At the bottom of the Brae was the Buy Well or Bowie Well Croft, and 'the Croft callit Roundabout' which in today's terms, probably stood near the Virginia Street/Castle Terrace/Commerce Street traffic lights. Other names that survive from the old records are the Powcreek Croft which adjoined Roundabout Croft, Tolmie's Croft 'in the territories of Footie' and Cryne's Croft which flanked the harbour side of the Summer Road. On the other side, marching with the Links were the Lang Rig, the Hede Rig and the Hill Croft. They were in Parson Gordon's words, 'fruitfull of corns, quheat, bear (barley) oats, pease and pot herbs and roots'.

In the distance, to the north east lay FootDee's Myre - that is how it is spelt in George Taylor's Plan of Aberdeen of 1773 - once owned by the Hammermen Trade. Here in 1682, James Gibbs, one of the greatest architects of the age was born into a Catholic, Jacobite family probably in the White House, shown in Taylor's Plan. Gibbs learnt his skills on the Continent, his patron being that Earl of Mar who had raised the Standard on the Braes of Mar in 1715, and a better architect than a general it seems. Gibbs settled in England where he designed St Martin's-in-the -Field and St Mary-le-Strand churches in London, the Senate House and the Gibb's Building in Cambridge, the Radcliffe Library in Oxford and much more. He gifted the design of the former West Church of St Nicholas to Aberdeen's magistrates in 1741, two years after being made a burgess. The south block of Seaton House in Old Aberdeen, which unfortunately succumbed to arson and was demolished in 1963 was also attributed to him.

South of FootDee's Myre stretched the Sandylands or 'Sandy Ground of Futt Dee' which much later was to give its name to the Sandilands Chemical Works. Conversely, the Summer Road, or Lane as it later became, lost its name in 1891 when John Miller, owner of Sandilands persuaded the Town Council to rename the ancient thoroughfare in his honour.

We have now reached 'the suburb called Fittie', *suburbe vocat fittie* to quote the original Latin of the Charter. Here Garvock Wynd, which ran from the Links to the Shorelands, effectively terminated the Summer Road by running across it at right angles. It was probably at this juncture that the Futty

Garvock Wynd in 1988. Fleming's Timber Yard, left, with its lum and Sandilands Chemical Works, right are both gone.

Gate was carried further east to 'the Haven, the Blockhouse and the Pier' by the Road to Pocra It also started from Garvock Wynd, but the traveller had to zigzag, walking a little way west along the Wynd to pick it up. Today Miller Street and St Clement Street, successors to the Futty Gate and the Pocra Road, join imperceptibly.

Garvock is said to be the same word as Garioch (Gaelic: a rough place), and in the late Middle Ages, the de Garvock family owned land on the Foty Gate. In 1357, Laurence de Garvock with John Crab and William Leith, was appointed Commissioner to the Scottish Parliament, and thus became one of the the city's first recorded MPs. De Garvock and his probable *alter ego* Laurence de Foty was Provost of Aberdeen in 1366-67, starting a tradition of Provosts with Fittie associations which survives to the present.

It was at 'Garvockis Wynd' that the magistrates discovered a blatant incident of purpresture - encroachment on the highway - when they perambulated and redded the Marches, in other words inspected and set in order the burgh's boundaries, in June 1599. (As magistrates were normally on horseback, redding was understandably corrupted to riding). On this occasion they discovered that Gilbert Black and Andrew Ewen who had land on either side of the Wynd had each 'labourit and takin in a pairt' within their own acres. They were ordered to 'desist' and the Dean of Guild was instructed to raise an action against them at the Court of Session. No pussyfooting about with threats of enforcement in those days. The reason for such draconian measures, however, related to the strategic postition of this highway. As the Charter of 1601 indicates, it led to Aberdeen's fort, the Blockhouse, the front line of defence against a sea-based attack. Along the Futty Gate and the Pocra Road the town's artillery was trundled 'in tyme of warre'. It was a matter of life and death that the highway be kept open for the passage of cannon and, as we will presently speculate, perhaps for men in a hurry as well.

When the alignment of the Summer Road and St Clement Street was improved during the earlier part of the nineteenth century, Garvock Wynd was truncated at their juncture and the old line westwards continued by Garvock Street. The latter has not survived but the Wynd is now a dreary lane which not so long ago separated Sandilands Chemical Works from Fleming's Timber Yard. Gilbert and Andrew would find it difficult to cultivate anything there now.

The 'suburb called Fittie' was well known as a fishing village, but there was more to it than that. At the upper end around Garvock Wynd and Footdee Church (St Clement's) was the Kirkton. Then came Middle Third, a narrow vennel with a dogleg in the middle and a cluster of cottages at the lower end. Middle Third ran at right angles from the Pocra Road down to the shore, in modern terms from St Clement Street to Waterloo Quay. It survived until the 1860s and was replaced by Lime Street a little to the east. Both the Kirkton and Middle Third were surrounded by open spaces and gardens. The Fish Toun of Footdee lay further east, shown on Parson Gordon's Map as two dozen cottages with enclosures behind. It lay in that stretch between Waterloo Quay and Clarence Street which is now occcupied by Seaforth Maritime.

The Pocra Road passed in front of the kirk as it still does. It continued behind the Fish Toun, not through it. This highway was not built for the convenience of the fisher folk. It then reached another sector of Footdee, the Pottery and the 'dockyards', the early shipyards, which were little more than small open yards and which even as early as Gordon's time, were developing along 'the Fishers Boate Haven or Pockraw '(later Pocra), the curving shore of the original harbour of Footdee. In modern times this area came to be occupied entirely by the Hall Russell shipyard. Beyond the haven lay journey's end, 'the Blockhouse and the Pier of Aberdeen'. It is difficult to estimate the antiquity of the latter. A pier doubtless replacing an older structure was built at Pocra in 1755 and as William Kennedy records in his *Annals of Aberdeen* (1818) 'was long known as the new pier'. This 'New Pear' appears in Taylor's Plan of 1773 equidistant from Pottery and Blockhouse.

There are many interesting features about the Fittie just explored. That it was a farming as well as a fishing community is clear from contemporary maps. From the mid-seventeenth century the Church was surrounded on three sides by its glebe, St Clement's Croft, and Parson Gordon shows cultivated rigs behind the Fish Toun stretching back to 'the Lynks of Futty'. The old records too indicate a number of contretemps involving the farming community. We have already met the two farming *purpresturistes* who were enthusiastically cultiving Garvock Wynd in 1599. The Council Register of 9 May of the same year also records the conviction of William Skene for punching ('striking in the breist with his neff'), Maister Robert Chalmeris who was ploughing in Futtie, and 'cutting with his knyff' the said Mr Robert's plough's traces, 'and staying (it) to gang'.

Roundabout Croft was also involved in an incident of purpresture in 1597 when the magistrates ordered a nearby encroachment on the highway 'passand towardis Futtie' to be 'instantlie demoleschit'. The need to rush ordnance to the Blockhouse was, as indicated earlier, perhaps not the only reason to maintain clear passage. Given that the road south over the Mounth was sometimes impassable, those who were impatient to leave Aberdeen were often better to do so by sea. It was not advisable, however, to embark from the Town's Quay at Shore Brae for the harbour estuary, in effect the sluggish outfall of the Denburn, had little depth of water and was navigable with difficulty even at high tide. On the other hand, though it did not compare with Torry as a deep water berth, Pocra could accommodate 'lesser ships' and was only a few minutes ride from the Castlegate. The strategic importance of the highway, and the fact that it ran behind the Fish Toun, not through it, thus affording an unobstructed route, now becomes apparent.

The pages of John Spalding's *History of the Troubles* 1622-1645 are peppered with desperate people leaving town in a hurry, and two episodes suggest that the pier could cope with significant numbers. In July 1639 Spalding notes that 'the nobles wold stay no longer in the toun, bot cam doun to Futtie'. They were accompanied by townsmen loyal to the King, armed with hagbuts (handguns) and muskets. The nobles supped in Futtie, 'and efter supper went aboard in their ain schipbottis', which suggests the presence of a small fleet. Three years later Captain Robert Keith and Captain Gordon 'schippit their solderis at Futtie; and upone the 5th of Marche, took up saill and gois to France, landing saiflie'.

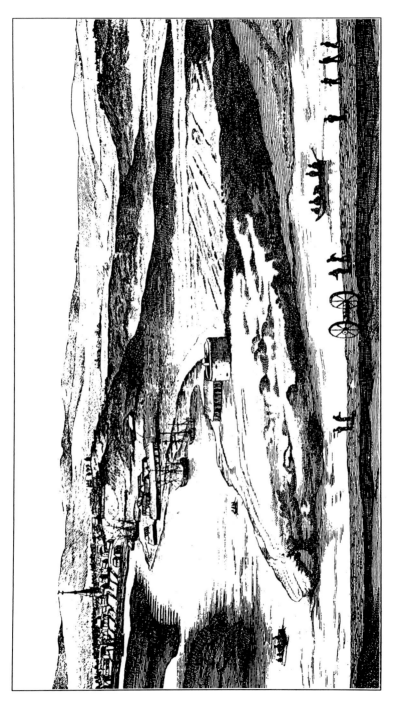

The circular Blockhouse, the fort of Aberdeen, is in the foreground. Behind lies the Pockraw (later Pocra) the haven of Footdee with two sizeable ships at anchor, and beyond that, the low thatched cottages of old Footdee. The Sandness promontory is in the front of the Blockhouse. It was here that today's Footdee and the North Pier were later sited. Note the lighter, left, making for port. Detail from New Aberdene from the Blockhouse by John Slezer, 1693

Chapter 2

The First Footdee

A godless and refractory generation
Aberdeen Council Register, 1600

A reference to the 'quhit fishearis (white fishers) of Futy' in the city records of the fifteenth century indicates that the Fish Toun was well established by that time, and was no doubt of much earlier origin. Ann Allardyce's monograph, *Footdee in the Eighteenth Century* , is a valuable record of village life in the 1780s but her description of the low, thackit cottages of the fishers might have been equally true of mediaeval times:

> Nothing could be more apparently comfortless than the exterior of these dwellings, each fronting the back of the opposite neighbour, and the narrow space between forming a line of dunghills, crossed over with supported spars from whence hung lines, bladders and buoys intermixed with dry skate and dogfish. The prospect was not more alluring to a stranger, and yet the inhabitants seemed quite contented. The earthern floor was dirty and uneven, the smoky roof whose only ceiling was a few old oars and pieces of driftwood..were objects far from pleasing.

The walls, she recalled, were bare, and inside there were only a few sticks of furniture, 'two clumsy black bedsteads...a small table, two or three chairs and some low seats or sunkies'. Fishing gear, 'lines, creels, sculls, murlans (baskets), formed all the rest of the visible moveables'. Sunday clothes were stowed in a chest and the saut-backet was suspended in the chimney.

Fishing dominated the life of the Fish Toun, but the fleet was was always small. In the eighteenth century there were never more than six boats, often less and sometimes none at all, for cholera, smallpox and dysentery made

Footdee from the Links. From left, the Blockhouse, now with crenellated battlement; the Fish Toun and Middle Third; St Clement's Chapel with belfry and steeply sloping thatched roof; extreme right, an inn, well placed to refresh the traveller from Aberdeen.
Detail from East Prospect of Aberdeen by Gregory Sharpe, 1732

fearsome inroads in such an enclosed community with primitive living conditions. Their harbour, the fisher haven, the gently curving bight at the Pocraw lying south east of the cottages is shown by Parson Gordon with the half dozen boats of the Fittie fleet either beached or at anchor there.

The Fittie men caught fish in season as the shoals came into the offing. In January and May, haddock was caught with the sma' line within sight of land. The great line season when cod, ling and turbot were caught 'sevin or aucht myles aff schoir' began in March, with the first occupant of a 'birth rowme' (berth room), a specific fishing station on March 1 keeping it for the season. An outbreak of tribal warfare inevitably followed. At a hearing of May 22, 1600 before the provost and bailies of Aberdeen, a number of complaints were laid against 'the inhabitantis of Futtie' for cutting or removing ropes both from stranger boats and local boats at the haven, no doubt to prevent rivals obtaining a favourable berth. Such vandalism was not new, but this outbreak seems to have been particularly vicious and the punishment likewise. 'Ony inhabitant of the said toun of Futtie, man or woman', caught at the 'wrangeous cutting' would be bound to a stake within the flood mark for three hours, while 'the water flow round about him', and then would be scourged through the burgh, and banished from Aberdeen. This did not act as a deterrent. The following March the magistrates complained, 'thair hes bene and is continewallie gryt trubil amang the fischeris of Futtie'. They fined William Williamson, master of Robert Fiddes's boat who had not only disputed Archibald Cadenheid's rightful 'berth', but worse still, with his four-man crew, had hauled Gilbert Main's great lines from his station, then hurled them into the sea 'in ane pairt far distant thairfra'.

Nor was Luddism unknown among the Fittie fishers. In August 1592 four whitefishers, Jon Nuckall (Nicol), Jon Hendersone, Alex Nuckall and William Cowye were fined for destroying an innovatory 'labster nett' which also caught 'partinis and paddillis (crabs and lumpsuckers) with uther sort of schelle fische' which Gilbert and Thomas Atholl also 'quhyt fischeris in Futtie' had set, round at Greyhope Bay. However the magistrates approved of the Atholl's lobster pot, 'ane necessar ingyne, and profitabill for the commoun weill' and threatened banishment if the offence were repeated.

The collecting of bait also produced its opportunists, and their activities were duly recorded in the Council Register. In September 1521, 'all and sindry' Fittie inhabitants were threatened with banishment for year and a day if caught removing mussels from a new skaup (bed), 'at the north watter, besyd the Cunnigar Hills', that is near the beach end of Pittodrie Stadium. The North Water, the old course of the River Don, used to curve south and flow into the sea beside the Broad Hill, an easy stroll for the Fittie mussel gatherers, though the womenfolk were known to walk as far as Balgownie when bait was scarce. Feuding went on for some years between the factor of 'my Lord

17

Abirdene', at that time William Stewart, Bishop of Aberdeen, who enjoyed the right to net salmon at the mouth of the Don, and 'the fyscheris of Futy', whose bait-gathering activities and interference with the fishing there had them threatened with incarceration in the Tolbooth. Matters were resolved in June 1541, when a code of conduct for the fishers was laid down. We learn the names of their leaders on that occasion: Geilis Monro, David Monro and John Collie.

The sixteenth and seventeenth centuries were lawless times in Footdee. In May 1600, the magistrates dealt with 'dyvers quarrellis' over enticing crewmen to change skippers without a term's notice; with Sabbath breaking; with penalties relating to non-payment of 'the just teind'. There were frequent arguments about the number and type of 'great fiches and small fiches' caught when calculating this tax. Two of Fittie's most unruly whitefishers of those days were William Brabner and Patrik Hutcheon. In March 1601 Brabner was banished from Footdee for pyckerie (theft), for which he had a number of previous convictions. He and Hutcheon, one of William Williamson's line-hurling crewmen, were convicted of cutting up and taking away 'ane gryt trie' from the Blockhouse, probably intended for the repair of the old fort. Their motive for the theft, perhaps for firewood or house or boat repairs, is not revealed. A year later Hutcheon was imprisoned in the Tolbooth for 'dinging' his neighbour, Barbara Leask.

There is also a record of violence towards non-residents. In 1558, James Allan and his wife were convicted of 'strublens, striking and blamaking', in a word mugging Marjory Paton of Monymusk 'under sylens of night within the toune of Futtie', and stealing her plaid, petticoat, two kerchiefs, a collar, a buckram apron, a stomacher and a pin cushion (preyne cod) which contained sixteen pennies so presumably it served as a purse. The bailies ordered that the Allans be placed in the stocks for twenty-four hours with feet fettered, doubtless after they had restored 'the said geir' which they were ordered to do within twenty-four hours. The Forbes of Monymusk and subsequently the Grants were superiors in Footdee and one might conjecture that the Allans - an early appearance of a common Footdee surname - had for some reason, perhaps because of a feud with their laird, taken umbrage at the grandly dressed Miss Paton.

Fittie men had to do their bit as members of the 'Home Guard', commanded by Parliament, for example, to muster on the Links in September 1611 along with the burgesses and craftsmen of Aberdeen. One phrase from the summons as recorded in the Council Register, 'the inhabitantis of Fittie with thair armour' seems to confirm that not all Fittie folk were fishermen. One cannot envisage fishers acquiring armour or having room for it in their simple cottages. Another, later occurrence that does relate specifically to fishers strikes one as unusual in such an enclosed tribe. In April 1746 four young whitefishers, John Duncan, John Main, George Wales and John Masson declared for the Young Pretender and marched to Inverness with Crichton of Auchingoul. The day before Culloden however, they 'deserted from the Rebels', and sensibly if not heroically returned home. They were imprisoned in Aberdeen's Tolbooth for their pains, 'until fuder orders'. Wolfe's Regiment of Foot had been quartered in the Town of Foot Dee' prior to Culloden so perhaps that had prompted the fisher lads to enter the fray on the opposite side.

As late as 1770 the Minute Book of the Footdee Society noted that the fishers 'do many times quarrel among themselves', but strife was perhaps on the wane. In that year there was a civilised approach to the mussel scaup in the harbour, the Fittie and Torry fishers leasing it for 10/- annually per boat, though the Cove men were banned. Physically too the village was expanding. Parson Gordon's single row of cottages of the late seventeenth century was replaced in George Taylor's Plan of Aberdeen of 1773, by half a dozen rows of cottages running from south west to north east, gable end to the sea.

The early Fittie fisherman was disinclined to go to sea except when the household purse was empty. However Aberdonians insisted on their fresh fish and in April 1591 the baillies ordained that the fishers would be 'poyndit', that is, have their goods seized, 'as oft as they remane aff the sey' providing 'wind and wedder' were fair. A lucky break came in December 1644 when there was a 'thundring out of pulpites' against celebrating the pagan festival of Yule. John Spalding reports: 'The quhytfisheris of Futtie was cammandit to go to sea on Yoolday under gryte pines'. Fortunately 'the sea fell out stormy', so they were able to stay at home and make merry.

Old Yule, Aul Eel, was celebrated on January 5. The boats were laid up, and the men, according to Ann Allardyce 'might be seen lounging at the gable end of the public houses playing at pitch and toss' while the women prepared for the feasts which were shared by each crew and their families. A delicacy called 'tyauen skate', dried skate, was served and, 'there was also a very large loaf baked with plenty of raisins and currants to which the happy faces of the children were constantly directed'. Roasted beef and mutton with broth were handed up from a pot by the fire as required, and 'a girded cogie and a pint stoup with one glass, were frequently handed round, and all seemed quite merry and delighted'. At the end of the festivites, 'doggy bags' were prepared. The broken meat and the remainder of the sweetie loaf were cut into equal portions, which the wives 'bundled it up in their aprons, and went home quite pleased and happy'.

A week later, at the time of the old New Year two ancient rituals were enacted at Fittie. On old Hogmanay, January 11, the cry, 'Burn the boat' went up and a bonfire of old boats and wood was kept going well into the night.

Later dying embers were carried round the houses to drive away evil spirits. This was a necessary precaution. In 1630, thirteen witches contrived the wreck of a Fittie boat at the Donmouth. (Today a similar ceremony, 'Burning the Clavie' survives at Burghead). The other ritual involved drawing the 'cream of the well'. Before midnight on Hogmanay a large crowd would gather round the village well, pushing and shoving to be the first to draw water after twelve o'clock which was believed to bring good luck for the year.

Fittie fishers along with their opposite numbers in Torry had sidelines as pilots and as smugglers, both perhaps more attractive careers than that of fisherman, though not without danger. Before the improvements which began in the later eighteenth century, the approach to Aberdeen harbour with its shallow, shifting inches or mud flats, was treacherous. As Parson Gordon commented: 'Nor dare any venture bot expert pilots, who can guide the way and have helpe of wind and tyde'. There were tragedies. Spalding recalls 'ane fishe boit of Futty' with skipper and a four man crew going out in 'in stress of wedder' in March 1640 to pilot in a Dundee boat. The skipper guided the vessel safely in to Aberdeen, but his crew returning to the Fittie haven in the fishing boat, met a sad fate: 'The boit perishes, thrie men drownis, and the fourth found with litle lyf'.

Pilotage of course, was not without its rewards and we can appreciate some of the financial benefits from the accounts of the Footdee Society, the whitefishers' Friendly Society which was in existence between 1761 and 1822. The pilots were also the masters of the Fittie boats and in 1771 the names of all five are noted: John Baxter, William Baxter, Robert Wales, John Duncan and Peter Main. As part of their contribution to the Society's funds, the skippers undertook on their own and crews' behalf, 'to pay unto the boxmaster for the use of the Society the odd twopence received by them of Pilotage of each Ship to and from the Harbour'. These 'odd twopences' usually accrued to around £6 sterling a year indicating a reasonable accumulation of pilotage dues. In 1801 we have a breakdown of all the Fittie pilots' names and the amounts paid by each into the funds

William Watson:	£2	5s	John Baxter:	4s	10d
Andrew Baxter:	£1	5s 6d	David Masson:	4s	8d
William Brand:		16s 10d	Andrew Allan:	4s	
Andrew Fowler:		14s 2d	Geo. Mason:		10d
Andrew Main:		5s 10d			

Fittie was well placed for the other lucrative sideline, smuggling. Large ships had to anchor in the deep water of the Gawpool between Pocra and Torry while their cargo was ferried by cabars - lighters of shallow draught - to the Town's Quay. This provided excellent opportunities for contraband goods, particulary wine and brandy, to be quietly landed at Fittie. In 1656, Thomas Tucker reporting to Cromwell on the cost effectiveness of the management of customs and excise in Scottish harbours struck an upbeat note:

'Both (Fittie and Torry) lyeing very neer unto the place where the ships usually ride....have given opportunity of muche fraud in landing goods privately, but prevented of late by appointing the wayters by turns to watching these two places narrowly when there are any shipping in Harbour'.

It is hard to say how effective these 'wayters'- tidewaiters or excisemen - were in the long run. Ann Allardyce writing over a century after Tucker's Report and as the daughter of the Footdee-based coastguard officer, well-placed to comment, notes that Fittie folk 'displayed a great share of cunning and firmness of purpose, along with apparent simplicity' particularly when being questioned about matters relating to contraband. She mentions one episode during the trial of a smuggler, which must have recalled memories of an eventful night at Fittie. The fishermen, were asked on oath: 'While the men were struggling in the water did you not hear the prisoner calling out, 'Drown the dogs, drown the dogs'? 'We saw nae dogs there, sir', was the evasive reply. So blasé were the fishermen about testifying at the Customs House that an oath of particular gravity was created. Its conclusion: 'If I do not speak the truth, and nothing but the truth, may my boat be a bonnet to me', with its overtones of death by drowning, 'touched on their superstitious fears,' wrote Mrs Allardyce, 'and was found to be far more effectual'.

Fishers, because of their precarious calling were highly superstitious, and Fittie folk were no exception. It was unlucky to count the boat's crew or the number of fish caught. No mention was made of minister, church or manse at sea so as not to offend the sea god by mention of the new religion. Salmon were referred to as 'red fish' and pigs as 'Sandy Campbell'. To avert bad luck there was a variation on 'Touch wood'. They said 'Cal iron' and touched metal or looked around for nailheads.

Mrs Allardyce gives a candid description of the Fittie fisherman as:

hardy and industrious, but ignorant in an incredible degree on all subjects unconnected with their own business. The elderly men wore broad bonnets, blue jackets and canvas kilts or short trousers. The younger men were rather good looking, smarter in their dress, and more good-humoured. They were indeed fond of music in as far as having a fiddle at their merry meetings, but their collection of songs was not extensive, consisting almost entirely of *The Praise of Paul Jones*, *The Woeful Ballad of Captain Glenn* and the Christmas Carol, *By Southend.*.

Perhaps there was a more varied range of music at Fittie weddings which were great festive occasions. Penny weddings where everyone who paid a shilling joined the guests were particularly popular in spite of attempts by the magistrates to prohibit them as unruly gatherings. The ceremony was carried out either in Footdee Church (St Clement's), or in the 'chamber', a small building with stone floor and iron-bound windows which is shown in the corner of the churchyard in some of the older maps. On its conclusion, the bridal party headed by a fiddler and a man carrying a flag in which to roll the bride crossed to a large tent in the loaning opposite. 'There was always an abundance of meat and broth served in broad pewter dishes', recalls Mrs Allardyce. After dinner, the traditional shame dance or shamit reel was danced on the Links by the bride, bridesmaids, groom and best man. The bride chose the music, (the shame spring), and the men each put a piece of money in the musician's hand. After this dance the guests 'returned and dispersed among the public-houses of which there were several at the ends of the lanes, where music and dancing were prolonged till a late hour...' meanwhile 'the young couple went to live in a house of their own and the poor girl got the creel to carry for life'.

Fishermen were married very young, and inevitably to girls from the fisher community. Few outsiders could have coped with the continuing drudgery of gathering bait, tipping and baiting the sma' lines, humphing heavy creels and selling fish as well as bringing up a family. In the earlier times, the Fittie wives had their stance below the Castlehill which was not too long a haul from the old village, and by no means as exhausting as trachling across from Torry or in from Cove with a huge creel. Later, however, they had to carry their wares up the Hangman's Brae to the market at the Fish Cross in the Castlegate.

The women aged prematurely and were bent by the creel. The traveller Thomas Pennant wrote in 1769: 'the *non plus ultra* of hard features is not found till you arrive among the fishwomen of Aberdeen'. In a lighter vein Ann Allardyce recalls the dress of the fisher folk. The middle-aged Fittie women wore 'a stuff gown with a large flowered calico wrapper or short gown over it, the young girls, a stuff wrapper and petticoat with the hair in a most unbecoming fashion. Boys under fifteen wore tattered hand-me-downs. Toddlers of both sexes, however, were quite charming in 'a simple dress of white plaiding, called a wallicoat which with their curly heads and rosy countenances, made them look very pretty as they puddled with their mimic boats'. The grandparents, Lucky-daddy or Lucky-minnie as they were called, lived with their sons or daughters. The grannies had a uniform of blue cloth hood or 'trotcosie' (throat cosy) and a man's coat with a large pouch by the side, a style that seems to have continued long in vogue. 'Elie Betty' a Fittie personality of a century later always wore, according to the 'East Neuk' chronicler William Skene, a head-dress and a man's jacket.

The house to which the newly married couple moved would perhaps be owned by the Footdee Society which acted as a housing agency as well as a Friendly Society, setting in tack (renting), houses to their own members. There is, for example, a sugggestion in 1793 that houses might be built for Andrew Fowler and Alex Baxter 2nd, two members who were about to get married. Most tenants were fishermen and a rent of £1 annually was the norm. The familiar Fittie surnames of that era predominate on the list of tenants: Wales, Main, Walker, Baxter, the latter being the most common. The houses were not rented exclusively to the whitefishers, however. Names such as Bridgeford and Swinton perhaps indicate the presence of wrights who had come north to give of their skills in the early days of shipbuilding. In 1777 the Society rented two houses to William McKinnen, 'Lighterman in Fittie' One of those dwellings might have been an inn since the Society held at least one of its annual meetings at a 'Mrs Mackinnon's at Footdee' (spellings are rarely consistent) as well as in other hosteleries, members houses, even, in 1756, at Footdeesmyre.

In 1793, the Society put forward plans to build seven new houses which would have been a great advance on the hovels described at the beginning of this chapter. These were to be 19ft by 15ft with a chimney in each and a partition wall. The roof and floor would be of homegrown wood, the doors and windows of foreign wood, all for £120. The mason, Robert Gill, had included the cost of tiles in his tender but the Society opted to thatch instead, with a saving of £20 10s. Gill was to receive £30 when the work was half done, the balance when it was complete. But the Minute records rather ominously: 'The Society authorises the Preses (chairman) Captain Gibbon to pay the money out of what he owes as it falls due....' In fact, these plans had to go completely on 'hold' in 1794. Far from paying Gill any money out of what he owed, the Captain had gone bust.

The Minutes explain that the housing scheme was 'not yet carried into execution owing to the bankruptcy of William and Arthur Gibbon who are possessed of the only funds the Society have for defraying the expense'. From time to time the Minutes make reference to a number of property deals with the Gibbon family, prominent members of the Society and of the Fittie elite who virtually ran the harbour and were involved in a number of mercantile enterprises at that time including the high risk business of whaling. The Society's funds seem to have been rather too closely linked to those of the Gibbons for comfort.

The Society's main function, however, was to support 'the Poor among us', the aged, the indigent, those 'unable to gain a livelihood or earn their bread by proper industry'. There usually numbered about fifteen annuitants receiving between £1 and 5/- and unlike the house tenants, benefits were strictly limited to 'the Poor of the Whitefishers actually residing in the Town of Footdee'. When a barber's widow appealed for charity in 1780, the Society pointed out she was not the widow of a whitefisher. She was reluctantly given 10/- 'but with this provision that she is never to get anything further from its funds'. The names of bona fide applicants usually remained on the list for a number of years. For a time, 'Geo Main's child' appears as do several women with the surname Leiper, one more usually associated with Torry. A more cheerful form of expenditure appears in later years under the heading of, 'paid to the Boys and drink as usual - 10/-'. This later changes to 'children and entertainments'.

The entry fee was a minimum of 2/6, though many gave more and some whitefishers paid only 2/-. Additional funding came from the annual subscription of 1/-, 'quarterly pennies gathered at the table', pilotage pennies, rent, bank interest, even fines payable by those who failed to attend meetings or promulagated quarrels.

The Society's membership provides a useful record of those who lived in or had Fittie associations during its lifetime. Of the eighty founder members in 1761, over thirty were whitefishers, but even then and in the years that followed, the spread of trades and professions was wide. There were gentlemen like the Gibbons and Captain Hugh Cochran, James Watson, advocate in Aberdeen and proprietor of Binghill, James Abernethey the Ferryhill ironmaster and James Chalmers, printer of the *Aberdeen Journal* with whom the Society placed advertisements. There were several 'writers' - lawyers who were not members of the Society of Advocates - as well as the schoolmaster, the minister, carpenters and wrights, mariners, a customs clerk, musician, goldsmith weaver, vintner, maltster, huxter, workman, watchmaker, barber, farmer, butcher and laxfisher (salmonfisher). While a number of these members would not have resided in Fittie, the majority did, showing that the 'suburb's' population was not entirely made up of fishers. Nor was the housing wholly composed of thatched cottages. Ann Allardyce refers to three slated houses which stood in the 1780s between Middle Third and the Kirktown. Her family, the Blairs, lived in one of those. A fourth near the Pottery was 'possessed by a respectable shipowner whose family then lived in a style of affluence and comfort not exceeded by the improvements of modern refinement'. Captain Arthur Gibbon perhaps?

Chapter 3

Relocation

In the year 1809 two courts of buildings were erected by the treasurer of Aberdeen for dwelling houses to the white fishers on the north side of the new pier where they now reside.

William Kennedy: Annals of Aberdeen, 1818

On 15 February 1808 three unusual petitions were placed before the magistrates of Aberdeen. Two were 'from certain pilots and fishers in Footdee' the third from 'the crews of *Nancy, Jean, Roger* and *Susan*, pilot boats belonging to Torry'. The petitioners stated that their houses were 'ruinous and uncomfortable' and that they had, moreover, been given notice to quit at Whitsunday which would be in three months time. The petitioners requested that the Town Council 'build Houses for their accommodation in the neighbourhood of the North Pier' for which they would pay a reasonable rent. Going on usual form the magistrates would either have prevaricated, declared that the petitions 'Be left on the Table' or dismissed them altogether. Instead they were accepted with considerable alacrity, the Council noting that it was 'very desirable and convenient to have their Pilots' places of residence somewhere near the Harbour mouth' and recording that ' the present Application which had come from the Pilots themselves offered a favourable opportunity of accomplishing that object'. This episode is out of character, both as regards the magistrates, normally given to procrastination, and the Fittie and Torry folk, rarely given to innovation.

A Committee of Petitions was now appointed to look into the proposed relocation and to procure estimates. In the intervening fortnight before the next Council sitting this Committee met 'repeatedly' and on 3 March 1808 reported that it would be 'exceedingly convenient to have Fishers and Pilots (at least as many as possible) stationed upon the north side of the River Dee'.

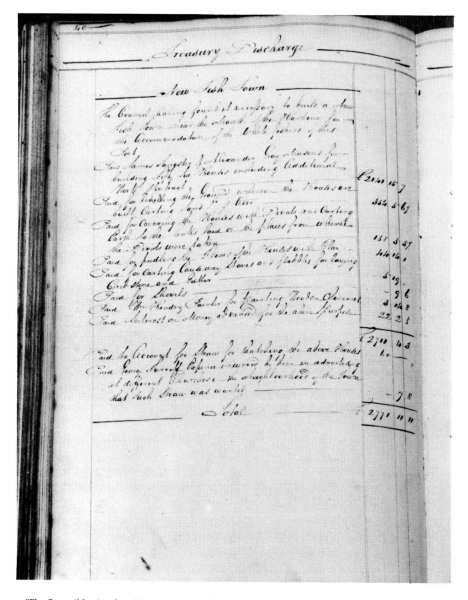

'The Council having found it necessary to build a new Fish Town near the Mouth of the Harbour for the Accommodation of the Whitefishers of this Port'. The account for the building of the New Fish Town from the Treasury Discharge of Michaelmas 1807-1808.
Courtesy, Aberdeen City Archives

A site east of the Blockhouse and adjacent to the North Pier was granted by the Town who owned much of the land at the far end of Footdee where it slopes south in the form of a promontory. On the older maps this continuation of the Links is marked as the Sandness, the headland of sand. The Committee of Petitions now recommended that the Council 'set about work without delay' to have accommodation ready by Whitsunday 'when very many fishers are warned to remove from their present dwellings'.

The Committee proposed laying out the ground in squares, each to contain twenty-eight houses one storey high, each house to accommodate one family. They had caused Mr. Smith, the Town's Superintendent to make out a plan of the ground and indeed this plan was already before the Council. (The previous June, John Smith, then only twenty-six years of age and already the architect of several distinguished buildings in Aberdeen was appointed 'Superintendent of the Town's Public Works in room of Mr Fletcher' - the latter gentleman having been largely resonsible for the engineering of Union Bridge). 'Sundry estimates' had already been procured and the tender submitted by the masons James Sangster and Alexander Gray was the lowest. Such, however, was the speed with which these plans were rushed along that no estimates were presented to the full Council. The Council Register shows gaps where the figures should have gone. Moreover the estimates referred only to mason work. No tenders had been obtained for thatching or for clearing and levelling the 'benty braes', the reed covered sandy hillocks of the Sandness.

Building work now quickly went ahead. The Treasury Discharge of Michaelmas 1807 - 1808 relating to the 'New Fish Town' - the spelling is now modern - reveals that the first phase cost £2771 11s 11d. Sangster and Gray were paid £2141 15s 7d for their mason work in building fifty-six houses. Levelling ground and carting sand cost £354 5s 6d. As it was springtime no straw was readily available for thatching and advertisements for 'A considerable quantity of dry and well drawn straw, payment 9d per stone' were placed in the *Aberdeen Journal* and George Turreff was paid 7/8d for 'Expence incurred by him in advertising at different Churches in the Neighbourhood of the Town that such Straw was wanted. (The Churches were likely to have been St Clement's itself, as well as Nigg and Newhills which were surrounded by fields). Divots were used as a stopgap roofing at a cost of £138 3s 5d which included 'Carting earth to the Links to be laid on the place from whence the Divots were taken'. The Links were clearly as sacrosanct, as they had been in the fifteenth century and this was a nice bit of environmentalism on the part of the magistrates. £44 14s 1d was paid for pudling the Floors of the Houses with clay' to make them watertight, and £5 19s 'for Carting Causeway Stones and Peebles for laying Cribstone (kerbstone) and Guttar', while the bill for shovels came to 9/6d.

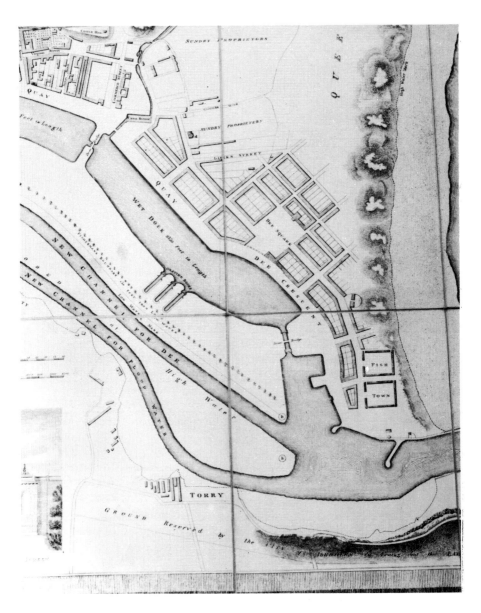

A detail from John Smith's Plan of Aberdeen of 1810 showing his stylish proposals for Footdee. Dee Square never materialised although the layout of surviving Fittie streets still hint at the elegant symmetry originally envisaged. Top centre, the building marked 'd' below 'Sundry Proprietors' was Footdee Church as built by Bailie Copland. 'Quay' and Dee Crescent became Waterloo Quay, and 'Wet Dock,' the Victoria Dock. The Fish Town, bottom right, is shown in its pristine state. Courtesy, Aberdeen City Archives.

The following year's accounts show that straw for the fifty-six houses had now been acquired at £189, and Williamson Smith was paid £72 10s for thatching. In their haste the Council had overlooked the provision of fresh water until petitioned by the inhabitants. John Blaikie, plumber, father of the Blaikie Brothers of whom more in Part Four, was paid £345 16s 5d for a leaden pipe for conveying water from a well at the Justice Port to the 'new fishing village'. In November 1808 William Hendry who had painted the wooden chimneys of the new cottages for £3 14s 8d the previous year continued his work and was paid £5 12s 8d for the doors and windows while Hugh Gordon received £2 3s 11d 'for hinges and snecks to the doors'. This second and final phase cost £726 3s 4d and the *Aberdeen Journal* reported that 'a neat and well laid-out new fish-town near the pier for pilots and white -fishers' was finished.

Planned villages were not an innovation in the North East. For nearly half a century Aberdeenshire lairds had lured weavers and other skilled workers to such settlements by offering benefits such as housing. They thus provided security and employment and at the same time increased the value of their estates. But an architect-designed New Fish Town, simple yet striking in style, built within the Inner Marches of the city at the behest of the Town Council was unusual enough in concept and style to excite comment. The lawyer-historian William Kennedy who was involved with the harbour area at this time in a professional capacity commented in his *Annals of Aberdeen* of 1818: 'In the year 1809, two courts of buildings were erected by the treasurer of Aberdeen for dwelling houses to the whitefishers on the north side of the new pier, where they now reside'.

Thirty years later Joseph Robertson recorded in the *Book of Bon Accord*:

Immediately in front of the Blockhouse is the Fish Town of Futtie erected by the Corporation at the begining of the present century. The houses which are neat and commodious are arranged in the form of two large quadrangles and are inhabited exclusively by fishermen and their families.

Thus Aberdeen's first planned council scheme came into being. Sturdy and stone-built, the cottages were a considerable improvement on the hovels of the old Fish Toun described by Ann Allardyce. But what was the real reason for the move? There was something odd about the original petition of the pilots and fishers who as it was already lived 'somewhere near the Harbour mouth'. As far as Fittie men were concerned their present dwellings though doubtless 'ruinous and uncomfortable' were on a relatively sheltered site. Why not request new houses to be built there instead of moving to the exposed Sandness and the full brunt of northerly gales?

We have to look at the progress of harbour improvements to find the answer. Between 1771 and 1781 the first phase of the North Pier had been built 'from a point called the Sandness', according to Mr Smeaton's plans. As a result harbour depths had been improved and access was now possible for larger vessels. To capitalise on this it was essential to build more quays for their accommodation and to provide a wet dock or basin, where ships could remain afloat at any state of the tide. As it was, many grounded at low tide and were damaged when attempting to refloat. And so in the 1790s plans were put forward by the engineer John Rennie for improving and enlarging the harbour,including the building of 'new Quays Wharfs and Docks'. A small wet dock was planned at Footdee. Although Rennie's plans were duly incorporated in the Harbour Act of 1797, they were eventually discarded as being too costly and on too small a scale. Nevertheless Footdee was irrevocably identified as the site for future developement and from the mid-1790s William Kennedy, wearing his lawyer's hat, had, at the Shoremaster's request, organised meetings of Footdee proprietors to discuss the implications of improving and enlarging the harbour. Some consequent movement of population must have been envisaged from this time.

The eventual impetus for action however was Thomas Telford's far-seeing Report of 1802. He stressed to the magistrates as had Rennie, the need for 'the greatest expanse of space for wharfs and wet docks, or basins where vessels may lie afloat at low water'. The shore of Footdee village, immediately west of the fishers' haven was earmarked for such a wharf and it was now essential for the Town to acquire the necessary ground. The year after Telford's Report, a Plan of Footdee was drawn up by the local surveyor Colin Innes, identifying the various proprietors. Among the Fish Toun landlords were four Baxters, four Wales who were shipmasters and whitefishers prominent in the village, and James Mackie, a shipmaster who appears from other documents to have owned his Footdee property in conjunction with Alexander Mackie, merchant, probably his brother. Their property lay along the shore of the Fish Toun. Additionally they possessed a large parcel of land between what would shortly become Wellington Street and York Place.

Their tenants, the Fittie fishers-cum-pilots would have to be removed. Yet it was to the magistrates not the landlords to whom these tenants appealed for new housing and it was the magistrates who took the sensible and humane step of providing for this highly valued elite. The remote Sandness, as already noted, was owned by the Town but was not required for harbour development. Accommodating them there must have seemed the ideal solution. There was, however, an element of the devious about the handling of the removal. The notices to quit would have been genuine, certainly in the case of the Fittie men, but the reason for these notices, the fact that the landlords had sold the ground their houses stood on to the Town is nowhere mentioned. There is no mention that homes will be demolished. No whiff of coercion is allowed to appear.

Had not 'the present application come from the Pilots themselves'? Whether or not some of the Fittie and Torry men were 'put up to it' is a matter for conjecture. Were there others who wanted to stay? We don't know. What is interesting from the comments of the Rev Alexander Spence is that there was a degree of consultation between the Town and the fishers which is not apparent from the Council Register:

> Each house consists of a but and a ben, with occasionally a small apartment between. The magistrates designed to have made the houses of two storeys, but the fishers refused to live up stairs and they refused to have any other than an earthen floor in their homes. In both of these though there may have been some superstition and a good deal of prejudice, there was also some reason for it would have been next to impossible for them to have kept a wooden floor clean, while an earthen one, if not clean, at any rate does not show the dirt so much, and it would have been very inconvenient for them to lug their long lines and their heavy baskets upstairs.

This hearsay evidence was probably accurate. Dr Spence's report is taken from the *New Statistical Account of Aberdeenshire* published in 1843 but he is known to have written it some years earlier.

The involvement of the Torry pilots in this saga now also becomes clear. With the development of 'wharfs and wet docks' planned for Footdee and the consequent berthing of numerous large vessels there, the importance of the deep water anchorage at Torry and in the Gawpool would diminish. Consequently the Torry pilots would, in modern parlance, miss out on job opportunities if they stayed across the water. Moreover it would seem sensible to have all pilots working from the same base. Four Torry pilots it will be recalled had petitioned for new homes at Footdee and they seem to have been successful. The accounts of teinds paid in 1808 show five fishing boats working out of Footdee and nine out of Torry. The following year ten were working out of Footdee with three left in Torry. If one goes by the skippers' names, at least three, perhaps four families crossed the water, including that of John Morrice, which explains why at this time we find a Torry name in Fittie.

Though the clearance of the old Fish Toun was important, it was by no means the only land deal that the Shoremaster Alexander Pirie was negotiating at Footdee on behalf of his fellow magistrates. Leases of houses and dockyards were restricted to short term which gave the Town flexibility and quick financial return, while landlords throughout the area were gradually bought out. In 1804, for example, houses belonging to George Simmers were acquired for £1194 and Charles, one of the Gibbon family received £550 for a dwelling. In 1806 the Shoremaster purchased ground belonging to Arthur Gibbon's Heirs for £210 and a house and ground belonging to Mrs Cumming for £350.

In 1808 Provost Ley's ground at Pocra was valued at £1000 by a jury empanelled by the Sheriff for such a purpose which he was happy to accept, though two other merchants Messrs Forbes and Hogarth, not content with a similar sum went to arbitration and were offered £800 more. The following year, William Yeats, the boatbuilder on the shore near the future Lime Street, received £1200 for his property and his advocate son George, laird of Auquharney, £550 for a house at Middle Third. The Footdee Society received from the Treasurer of Aberdeen a bill (an early form of cheque) for £1841 1s, ' as part of the price of the subjects in Footdee sold by the Society to the Town', as well as £40 in cash. To determine the compensation the jury had 'perambulated and inspected the subjects' accompanied by Society officials who 'did everything in their power to obtain the highest sum possible for the Society'. Altogether the compensation offered by the Council appears to have been generous, particularly that offered to Robert and Alexander Mackie who in 1806 not surprisingly declared themselves well satisfied with £4400 offered by the Shoremaster for their 'Houses, Tenements, Riggs,Yards Butts of Land....'

The description of the Mackie's property gives a hint of that other, more gracious Footdee which is briefly glimpsed in Ann Allardyce's monograph. The deed refers to a number of properties including a large house with a large ridge or garden, a house formerly belonging to Sir Archibald Grant of Monymusk, 'a large tenement lately built with Stone and Brick, covered with Tyles and Butterage (buttress) or Stone Fence erected before the Door to defend the same from the Tides....' Herein lies the clue to the Shoremaster's generosity. The Mackie's property lay on land earmarked for the future Waterloo Quay and its acquisition was essential to the impending development of the harbour, but it would appear that the Mackies still retained land in Footdee outwith the area destined for developement. In 1837, the blacksmith William Simpson negotiated the feu duty of the land between Wellington Street and York Place, where the future Hall Russell engineering shop would be built. It was at that time according to the Council Register still 'occupied by Alex Mackie Jnr'.

The Act to secure Telford's harbour improvements was obtained in 1810 and the following year work started on a new wharf, the future Waterloo Quay, 'upwards of 900ft in length running along the south side of Futtie', as Kennedy described it, running in fact where the houses nearest the shore had stood. The quay was specifically constructed to support the projected wet dock, the future Victoria Dock on which so much of the harbour's wealth would depend. Summing up harbour developments William Kennedy commented on the construction of the North Pier as well as 'considerable operations....upon the Inches, preparatory to constructing the projected graving docks, and the interior of the harbour has been deepened and many obstructions removed by means of a powerful dredging machine which is in constant operation'. Nevertheless as he grumpily recorded in his *Annals* :

In the execution of these extensive works and in the purchase of considerable property in Futtie for account of the harbour, a debt of upwards of £127,000 has been contracted, although the grand and primary objects of the design being the tide lock, basin and graving dock have not been accomplished. A contrariety of sentiment still prevails among many intelligent men on the subjects of these improvements.

And as Kennedy was writing, development at Fittie, both industrial and residential, complementing the mighty harbour works was going on apace. Part of the area was neatly indicated in red ink on Colin Innes's Plan of 1803, encompassing St Clement Street and Waterloo Quay to the north and south, intersected by Clarence Street and Lime Street. Today, the hand of John Smith the Town's Superintendent is apparent not only in the original sturdy simplicity of the 'new Fish Town' but in the area between it and Wellington Street where the streets, though flanked by rundown remnants of earlier industrialisation are still spacious enough to be virtual boulevards. Shipbuilders and shipyard managers lived comfortably in Wellington Street dating from 1816, in York Street which replaced the old Pocra Road in the mid 1820s, in York Place dating from 1830 as well as on Waterloo Quay itself. A handsome building by John Smith still surviving at the south end of St Clement Street

This fine building was designed by John Smith in the 1820s for combined residential and commercial use. Several prominent shipbuilders lived here. It still stands at the south end of St Clement Street indicating the handsome nature of his plans for the harbour area which unfortunately were never fully realised.

was designed for both residential and commercial use. The scenario was similar in the developing suburb of Ferryhill with industrialists living a few minutes ride from their foundry or brewery. Aberdeen's west end was still years away, and living virtually 'over the shop' was the accepted mode for master and worker alike. Unfortunately Smith's plans for a fine harbour hinterland were never fully realised.

In conclusion, one cannot help wondering what were the feelings of the fisherfolk in their 'neat' though scarcely 'commodious' new homes? They had been so precipitously resettled on the barren headland of Sandness that no fresh water was available, nor was there straw to thatch the cottages. Wedged as they were between the two shore batteries erected in the early 1780s, the Footdee Squares would have been a prime target had the feared Napoleonic invasion ever materialised. Unpleasant realities included the foul stench from the boilhouses standing in a close-set row behind the Fish Town where whale fat was rendered into oil every autumn and winter; a lengthier trek to the Castlegate with heavy creels for the women folk; noise from continuous work on the second phase of the adjacent North Pier between 1810 and 1816 which must have made a building site of the area; and periodic incursions from the North Sea which brought flooding and devastation until relatively recent times. In September 1993 the flood gate at Footdee was closed to prevent possible damage when a particularly high tide was anticipated due to the full moon coinciding with the autumn equinox.

As for old Footdee, it did not vanish overnight, at least not completely. The 'Houses called the Kirktown', safely inland beside 'the Head of Garvock's-wynd' survived well into the nineteenth century and were a shoreporters' staging post. Some of the old fisher homes, presumably those furthest from the shore were recalled in 1896 by Lord Provost Mearns who had been born in 1840, and brought up nearby in Yeats Lane off the Summer Road. He still remembered 'the two steps down, and the earthen floor....' Did the womenfolk ever look back with nostalgia as they tramped past with laden creel?

Chapter 4

Footdee in Modern Times

We brak nae breid o idecy
Doon bye in Fittie Square
A' Night oor men toil on the sea
An wives man dee their share

Anon

The two new Fisher Squares at the Sandness were completed by 1809. There were by then ten boats working out of Fittie, some crewed by Torry incomers. If there were six men to a boat and fifty-six cottages available offering single family occupation as ordained by the magistrates, there would seem to be more families than houses even from the begining, although a number of crew members would presumably have been unmarried sons living at home. But just as the planned villages of the North East attracted skilled workers from a wide area, so the new Fish Town, which combined the advantages of working out of Aberdeen with a handily placed new house at a reasonable rent, drew whitefishers from Cove, Burnbanks, Portlethen even Collieston. Guyan has long been a well known Fittie surname but it was probably at this time that the Guyans, previously based in Cove, settled there. The name is Norman French in origin and the Guyan tribe is particularly far flung. Guyana in South America and the Vietnamese name Nguyen are all thought to derive from the same root.

In the early years cholera was an unwelcome visitor as it had been in the old village. Joseph Robertson reported that in the Squares in 1832 nearly one in every twenty was carried off compared with less than one in eight hundred in other parts of the city. In 1833 petitions were presented to the Council over the state of the drains and John Smith was instructed to take action 'with a view to remedying the evil'.

When the Squares were only quarter of a century old, William Philip,

The 'gap site' house on the west side of South Square

Middle Row facing North

Master of Kirk and Bridge work reported to his fellow councillors that many of the fisher houses were in bad repair and overcrowded. Additional accommodation was urgently required. This demand continued and in August 1837, John Smith, now 'the Town Architect' accompanied by the City Chamberlain set off on a site visit. Smith drew attention to the open space in the middle of the west side of each Square, clearly visible on his Plan on Page 28. He suggested that one house be built in the middle of this 'gap site' still leaving passage room, and that in addition, the Squares be divided into two equal parts by a range of seven houses running east to west. It was then decided that eight houses in the south Fisher Square 'will be quite sufficient in the meantime and when more are required the like number can similarly be built in the other Square'. The houses were to be of one floor, substantially built, tiled and the tiles covered with coal tar, with eaves of slate. Each house was to cost £50 and they were to be 'erected with all convenient speed'. Thus Middle Row in South Square came into being, nicely designed to confuse the uninitiated with numbering starting in the centre with Nos 1 - 3 facing north and Nos 4 - 7 facing south. The plan was never repeated in North Square the afore-mentioned gaps being filled by educational and ecclesiastical establishments.

Problems of overcrowding and contagious diseases went on unabated. In 1849 a committee was set up specifically to see to 'the improvements of the Fisher Squares' while in 1854, during another epidemic James Hall the public-spirited shipbuilder wrote to the Town Council expressing his concern about overcrowding and suggested 'the erection of another Square of Houses of a better description'. Pilot Square, a row in spite of its name was subsequently built at the south end of South Square, the house to a substantial design of

Pilot Square

37

hammer blocked rubble work with an upper storey now permitting official multiple occupation.

Three accounts of the village in the middle years of the nineteenth century reveal certain changes in lifestyle. Firstly Dr Spence, minister of St Clement's parish, notes in the *New Statistical Account* of 1843, that fishermen working as pilots would earn between £1 10s and £2 weekly during summer, and were able to make fully as much as 'any other labourers in the same class of society'. He adds disapprovingly: 'At the same time their double employment as fishers and pilots is by no means favourable to their religious, moral and domestic habits'. The women as of yore kept the money from the sale of fish though, 'it is not often that either party manages these gains to the best advantage'. Drunkeness he noted was prevalent though not universal, and as a rule, the fishers were hard-working and extremely honest, while their houses, generally speaking, were 'as clean and comfortable as the nature of their occupation will admit of'.

In *Fishing Boats and Fisher Folk* (1930), Peter Anson paraphrases comments made by James Bertram in the 1860s which confirm the fishwives role as the holders of the purse strings:

Those Footdee men were a much poorer class taken as a whole than the rest of their brethern. Their boats were old and they never ventured far from shore. It was the womenfolk of Footdee who ruled the community in those days. The young girls or 'queans' baited the lines and carried the fish to market. The older women sold the fish and kept a strong hold on their earnings. In fact the men had nothing to do but catch the fish. Just now there are many fishermen who will not go to sea as long as they imagine their wives have got a penny left from the last hawking excursion. The women enslave the men to their will and keep them enchained under petticoat government.

Finally a cheerful account from an unidentified local journalist of the 1860s is quoted by Bertram:

We have visited both Squares of Footdee, and found the interior of the houses as clean sweet and wholesome as could be desired. Their whitewashed walls and ceiling, their well-rubbed furniture, clean bedding, and freshly sanded floors, present a picture of tidiness such as is seldom to be met with among classes of the population reckoned higher in the social scale. And this external order is only the index of a still more important change in the habits and character of our fisher-town, the population of which has within the past few years undergone a remarkable change for the better in a moral point of view.

And the anonymous journalist goes on to praise the great improvement in educational standards of the fisher children. If we can draw a conclusion about developments in the years between the Spence and Bertram commentaries, it is firstly, that by the 1860s Footdee had progressed to being a better educated, more sober community. The improvement in learning can perhaps be attributed to the higher standards set by Alexander Brownie, the then head of Davidson's School, founded exclusively for fisher children. As far as sobriety was concerned, the great religious revival of the 1860s that swept the Fisher Squares had gone a long way towards putting an end to drunkeness. On the other hand, Bertram's comments that Fittie fishermen were 'a poorer class' does not sit well with Spence's earlier account of the pilot/fisherman and his double wages. In the intervening years between these reports, however, an increasingly sophisticated harbour system had been created. Victoria Dock, the long-awaited wet dock was completed by 1848. In the 1850s, the government began to introduce new regulations regulating pilotage, commencing with the Merchant Shipping Act of 1854. Piloting was skilled work and not all fishermen now doubled as pilots and enjoyed a double income. Indeed the naming of the most southerly 'square' as Pilot's (the singular apostrophe was later dropped), would indicate the arrival of the pilot as a separate entity. It could be that Bertram had detected an 'underclass' of less skilled, and thus poorer fisherman who would not or could not undertake pilotage duties in a harbour that was changing out of recognition.

What had not changed was overcrowding in the Fish Town. Acccording to Bertram, in the late 1860s, sixty-four two-roomed single-storey houses, that

The Tower of Babylon c1900 which with the two houses, centre, replaced the Free Kirk School. Compare the same scene today on the front cover

39

The tall tenemental additions to the east side of Pilot Square

is the original fifty-six plus the eight of 1837, accommodated 584 inhabitants, giving nine or thereby for each two-roomed house. Apparently in both North and South Squares only three houses were now occupied by a single family, which had been the magistrates' original ideal. Most buts and bens were shared by at least two families with one small room apiece, while four single rooms in North Square contained two families each.

During the 1860s and 1870s, however, various improvements were introduced. One was for a more ample water supply with tenants contributing £8 towards the expense of laying down piping for two wells. Another scheme was for better lighting. In 1870 the fishermen and pilots wrote to thank the Council for 'the recent improvements at the Squares'.

In fact 1870 was a particularly busy year for building in and around the Squares for once again the magistrates were attempting to impose the one-house-one-family rule. It could not be enforced, however, until more accommodation was provided. William Smith, architect of Balmoral Castle who was following in his father's footsteps as City Architect, was in charge of developments. The Free Church School which had filled the 'gap site' in North Square rather than housing as originally envisaged, was taken down and replaced by three new two-storey four-roomed houses, using stones from the school. These houses are illustrated as they are today on the cover of this book. Pilot Square was extended though in a rather curious fashion. In 1870 three tenements were planned for the east side and a further three followed on the

40

west side in 1873. However Pilot Square retained its pristine condition as a row of two-storey houses while these tall tenemental additions were tacked on to the east and west sides of South Square.

Matters had been eased a little in the February of that year of 1870 when the shipbuilders Walter Hood & Co. relinquished land south east of the Ferry Boat Inn 'for development of fisher housing' and were complimented by the Council for their generosity. James W Barclay, the Master of Shoreworks and subsequently one of the city's MPs is given credit for this development of a row of tenements in what became New Pier Road. The first three to be built were to house eighteen families all told, in six flats per house, with three rooms for each family and water laid on. A fourth, also part of this scheme followed soon after, while four years later in 1874, plans for yet another dwelling house at New Pier Road were approved, probably No 5 which is different from the others. For many years the ground floor housed one of the small shops in the area. In addition the Council set about improving the extant housing stock, though a request in 1870 to have an Engine House near the bents, just north of North Square converted for use as 'dwellings for workmen' was declined. In spite of continuing problems of overcrowding, the Council seemed determined to retain the Squares as near their original state as possible and to prohibit any attempt to fill them with housing. Perhaps we have William Smith to thank for this early attempt at conservation, anxious that what little

New Pier Road. No 5, right, is later than the others and was once a corner shop

41

of his father's plans for Footdee that had been implemented should at least be preserved. In 1878 the Council declined the request of David Fowler of 14 North Square who wished to feu ground to build a house beside the Mission Hall while the following July they threatened legal action to remove fisher families who had set up shanties between the Squares.

July is highly relevant, the month when the herring season was at its height. Following improvements, Aberdeen harbour was able to accommodate the herring fleet of over 400 boats and its accompanying gutters, packers and coopers who came to Aberdeen in their thousands during the summer seasons between the early 1870s and mid 1890s. Point Law was crammed with farlans or curing yards while others were established at Pocra. The herring fleet auxiliaries gravitated to the Squares for accommodation in spite of the fact that handbills were circulated by the authorities, threatening legal action if houses were found to be overcrowded or if footways were obstructed by herring barrels. One suspects such prohibitions would have been to no avail. This influx, of course, was in addition to the 200 or so fishers now permently resident in Footdee. By the late 1870s, the ten boats of the fleet of 1809 had grown to around ninety and about half of these were big enough to make the conversion from line to net as the herring season followed the white fishing.

Another solution to the overcrowding problem was presented in 1878 when the architect Duncan McMillan, representing a consortium, received permission to erect fisher housing on ground occupied by the Footdee Sawmills, one lot 'for the erection of a better class of house' fronting York Street, and 'on the eastmost portion of the ground....a square of houses of the cheaper kind'. These never materialised and the Footdee Sawmills were still going strong until the mid 1930s. Some years after McMillan's plans, however, a large house and a row of red-tiled white-washed brick cottages, thought by the locals to be haunted, were built in York Street beside the sawmills. This little enclave was known locally as Coullie's Opening and it was used as a short cut to the Links.

It was in the 1870s that the Council began to evolve a new policy towards the Fisher Squares. One can't help feeling that in these days, before housing departments were dreamed of, the magistrates were not yet geared to cope with the hassle of running a council scheme with the endless requests for accommodation and housing repairs. The fishers, it was decided, would now be given the opportunity to buy their council houses. There is nothing new under the sun. The civic coffers would profit by the ready cash, and the Fittie folk would be left to dree their ain weird. First to be sold off, in July 1870, were the new 'extremely plain but substantial and commodious' tenements at New Pier Road which had cost just over £1000 to build. The flats went for £75 each which should have brought in a profit of almost £800, though payment by instalment was permitted. The east side additions to Pilot Square too were

North Square, showing the original single-storey level and the exposure to the sea.

rouped after completion as were their opposite numbers which later appeared on the west side.

The Council Registers of the 1870s also contain a number of reports of the repair of houses as well as their sale. In 1874 for example four houses on the west side of the south Fisher Square were to be reroofed with slates and the floors laid with cement. The rents would be from £4 to £6 annually. A sensible policy of repair first then sell was adopted with regard to the older houses and virtually the last batch went on the market at the end of 1880 when thirty houses were offered in five lots. The upset price of the first lot, the oldest cottages, was £65 and they fetched between £85 and £103. Only one house was offered in the second lot and it sold at £107, £2 above the upset price. A further six houses comprised the third lot and they sold from between the upset price of £120 and £150. Fourteen houses were originally offered in lot four and seven were sold at prices from the upset of £120 to £150. Seven, however, Nos 8 - 14 North Square were withdrawn. They caught the full force of the North Sea and had to wait until the bulwark was reinforced. The 'propriety of reducing the upset price' was also discussed. Lot Five, six houses in Pilot Square all went for the upset price of £180. These prices compare interestingly with those of the early 1990s when the same dwellings, 'much altered' internally, with attractive, modern interiors are fetching £80,000 and more. The new home owners of the late nineteenth century were allowed to pay by instalment over a twelve year period. A few years later, however, the Council was chasing backsliders to recover arrears.

After the roups of the 1880s, the Squares became an enclave of owner occupiers and a spate of independent rebuilding got underway. The overall effect is one of attractive idiosyncrasy, on which the masonry and symmetry of the Squares impose a sense of uniformity. Although patches of single storey houses remain, several at this time 'grew' to two or three storeys and nowhere more dramatically than at the 'Tower of Babylon' as it was subsequently nicknamed which sprouted to four. It is the northmost of the three houses in North Square which replaced the Free Church School in 1870. It was bought as a single storey by one of the pilots who extended it upwards over the years to accommodate his growing family. In South Square No 17, the home of Mr John Gillanders, bears the date 1894, evidence of a very thorough rebuilding at that time.

The famous, nay notorious tarry huts which some say give character to the Squares, others argue are an affront to the stone culture, had started to appear by the mid-nineteenth century and by 1870, were being supplied along with the new houses, much as garages are today. They were used originally to stow fishing gear and subsequently served as washhouses, water closets or for storage. Some still have little glass boxes perched high, containing a model boat, some have been replaced by later models, but by and large they continue in multi-purpose use and in individualistic array.

The Town Council in the later nineteenth century also extended the water supply providing half-a-dozen wells in the Squares which until relatively modern times were used, among other things, for rinsing the clothes on washing day. The soap suds kept the broad causeyed gutters clean. The wells are handsomely maintained but frost damage has now effectively ended their lives as working wells. The Council apparently are not able to undertake reinstatement on health grounds. A number of latrines were also provided for the male population and Mrs Ruby Webster who has spent a lifetime in the village recalls how the old fishermen would stroll along to the one by the gap between the two Squares to enjoy the view out to sea and a quiet smoke of an evening only to be pestered by mischievous loons climbing on the roof and throwing down bits of lighted paper.

Other amenities came, slowly. In 1895, the Council 'reluctantly' granted permission to Fittie residents to use the ground behind John Rust's Footdee Sawmills for the purpose of practising athletic sports, on the understanding that 'football playing is not allowed'. This seems a little grudging in view of the fact that Aberdeen was enjoying at that very moment the great era of public parks. However, the land behind 'Roosties' was none other than the sacrosanct Links. In 1906, a further concession was gained when a piece of ground was acquired as a bowling green.

In and around the Squares, however, multiple occupation remained the norm well into the twentieth century. The Tower of Babylon for example at one time housed three families with the owner on the ground and top floor, two other families living in between and a communal sink on the landing. Ruby Webster of South Square recalls her grandfather's house at No 8 where he and his family had one room while the other was occupied by his brother, wife and daughter. The attic was made use of 'but they were packed top to tail like herring in a barrel.' There is also a tradition which still survives of sisters sharing a house, the menfolk having originally married into the Square. According to John Gillanders who married into North Square over sixty years ago but is nevertheless an 'incomer' from Links Street, 'they never liked men coming into the Squares to take away the women.' This is a throwback to the work pattern that existed from the very earliest days when women were needed to shell the mussels, bait the lines, and sell the fish. That tradition survived until relatively recent times. Ruby Webster's mother, Roberta Murray, nee Baxter, and a cousin would take the ferry to Nigg to gather buckies and dulse to sell in the Castlegate. Mrs Webster, now in her early

Mrs Roberta Murray braving the elements as she hung out her washing.
Courtesy of Mrs Ruby Webster

Mrs Ruby Webster

Members of two traditional Footdee families, from left, Mrs Jessie Walker, George Walker and Mrs Thelma Cowper. Courtesy, Robert Smith.

seventies, recalls getting a piggy back home in a creel at the age of three or four, just able to peep over the edge. She still remembers her grandmother in traditional fisher dress, a murlan on her arm and her creel on her back.

'It was,' says Mrs Webster, 'a great community in our young days.' The family have always had an organ which her mother used to play and there were singsongs of an evening. There would be gatherings at her grandfather's with the children on a long bench by the fire where the big iron kettle hung, listening to his tales. One favourite community activity was a trip to the beach to gather coal. This was in the old days of coal-fired steam trawlers when numerous pieces of coal, even whole bags would accidently fall into the harbour during coaling. The harbour dredger the faithful old *Annie W Lewis* regularly dredged up these coals which were later dumped out in the Bay. 'Lovely coals would be washed up on the beach when the tide was right,' recalls Mrs Webster. 'A crowd of us went along to collect them, not because we were hard up, but we got such a laugh together, wading in, pretending the water wasn't cold.'

One piece of coal that was of particular importance was the lump given at First Fittin at Hogmanay. It would usually be left in the home all year, recalls Mrs Webster. The houses were cleaned from top to bottom at this time. Andrew Baxter in his memoirs *Bygone Days of Footdee* mentions another old custom in which the young folk smeared the windows with sowens so that on Ne'er Day morning every window in the village was white. This custom does not seem to have been revived after the First World War.

Superstitions regarding weddings also survived into the twentieth century. Andrew Baxter, whose memoir dates from the immediate post-war period recalls that on Fastern's Een, Shrove Tuesday, young women would place a tumbler of water with the contents of an egg on the window sill. Whatever shape the contents took during the night denoted what kind of a husband the young woman would get! Soldiers and policemen at that time were not in favour as potential husbands. 'Whatever the reason, I don't know', Baxter added, 'but both classes are now represented in the married life of the village'. He recalls the feet-washing night and the bed- making ceremony the day before the wedding, a fertility rite, when only women whose husbands were alive could attend, while the woman who made the bed had to have a large family. Ruby Webster recalls that flags were taken from the boats to decorate the village 'overall' on the occasion of a wedding.

A red-letter day in her childhood and for everyone in the Squares was the Fittie Picnic, organised by the Mission Hall's committee. 'Nobody could sleep the night before because of the excitement. My mother got the older ones ready first and was always worried in case they got dirty while the younger ones were having their baths. We had bows in our hair and maybe new frocks made from material from 'Raggie' Morrison's. It would cost about 1/11d. We were up and dressed by seven though things didn't start till nine. There was great excitement when the Oakbank School Pipe Band arrived on the scene. There would be a prayer and a hymn or two in the 'Schoolie' and fizzy drinks for the Oakbank boys. We formed up behind the band and and marched two or three times round the Hall, then off up to the Joint Station. When we marched up York Street the shipyards stopped and the men came out to see us off.' The Picnic was usually at Milltimber. She recalls a terrible storm one year, and the large hats of the women all drooping in the rain. 'We were all dead tired when we got back. In my days we always went by train, but in my daughter's day they went in six double deckers.'

Mrs. Webster recalls one of the Fittie ladies who always wore a particularly large hat being nicknamed 'Princess Mary'. With so many people related and sharing a handful of surnames - Allan, Baxter, Brand, Caie, Fowler, Guyan, Main, Noble - tee names (though not normally aristocratic ones), were necessary to distinguish the residents. 'Boolies Ondy', a fisherman was an Allan, 'Bowfer' a skipper, a Baxter; 'Sheepie' and 'Hodge', a Noble and a Caie were pilots; 'Pokie's Dod' was a Baxter as was 'Foveran's Ondy'- the chronicler Andrew Baxter of Mission Hall fame. There was Annie Baxter One, Annie Baxter Two, 'Tootsie's Minnie', 'Tarrie's Nellie' (John Gillander's mother-in-law), 'Tady's Ondy', 'Lang Willie', 'Cove Sandy' and 'Velvet Boots'. Mrs Webster's mother, one of the great Fittie personalities was 'Tony's Robbie' (for Robertina). Mrs Webster herself is 'Rommel's Ruby' and when her mother got drift of this nomenclature she said, resignedly, 'Oh weel, I'm ca'ed efter a great man onyway'. John Gillanders is 'J G'.

As well as multiple occupation, lack of modern conveniences remained well into the twentieth century. Ruby Webster recalls that in the immediate post-war era those who had become tenants in the new council estates felt a sense of superiority because they had bathrooms. Sizeable public toilets that appeared at this time at the Fittie end of the Esplanade were convenient for the locals as much as for those visiting the Beach. Fittie residents however, were now understandably seeking planning permission for bathrooms and extensions. The city planning department was equally anxious to see modernisation though not in a piecemeal but in a uniform way that would retain the original character of the village. In 1968 the Squares were designated a Conservation Area and two years later an exhibition staged at the Beach Ballroom showed how the cottages could be appropriately upgraded with the construction of half houses at the rear to provide bathroom and kitchen, at the same time preserving the original roofline. Improvements would cost around £1000, with grant aid covering half.

Mr and Mrs Webster's home on the east side of North Square, one of those which still remains at single storey level, is an example of how neatly this has been carried out. The original house, a but and ben of two rooms where two families would once have been encamped is now sitting room and bedroom. The modern part to the rear contains a bathroom and kitchen with dining area, and offers a superb view of the 'Fittie Links' and the sea. There was some disappointment, however, when these 'half houses' were added to the seaward cottages. Construction work affected the view and familiar landmarks such as the Cave Rock disappeared. The Squares were also landscaped to allow the creation of gardens while the old lifeboat sheds were cleared away from behind South Square. In 1970 a children's playground was laid out behind Pilot Square. John Gillanders can remember the women sitting together near there of a summer evening with their knitting. 'It was the most friendly place. Folk in the past could name every single resident.'

In spite of all good intentions there was consternation in the planning ranks in 1982 when it was discovered that out of the ninety-three Category B listed buildings in the Squares, around fifty had been altered without planning permission, and twenty-two of these alterations did not meet the necessary standards, some having acquired what was regarded as unsuitable modern doors and windows. Some residents whose homes had been handed down by their forebears did not take particularly kindly to planning directives while for their part, the planners may well have agreed with the magistrates of 1600 in pronouncing the Fittie folk 'a godless and refractory generation'. Since then,

The Pocra Quay play area.

49

however, inappropriate modern embellishments have been replaced and a particularly happy development has been Mrs Helen Clark's thoughtful and painstaking restoration of the Tower of Babylon which had lain derelict for fifteen years before she bought it in 1981.

In the early nineteenth century the Squares were attractive to their original inhabitants because they were so near the harbour. Living virtually 'over the shop' continued into the post-war era when the village had fifty or sixty working fishermen, and many of the menfolk like Ruby Webster's husband George were employed in the shipbuilding industry. Her father, a cooper, had worked nearby at the cooperage down the road at Pocra Quay. Billy Cowper and George Walker, neighbours in South Square, continued this tradition, both working as harbour boatmen and serving as lifeboatmen like their fathers before them. They too are traditional Fittie families. George's wife Jessie is a Walker from North Square though Thelma Cowper like John Gillanders is an

'incomer' of long standing from Links Street. Billy Cowper and George Walker are the last in an old tradition of living virtually 'on site'. Sadly with the deaths of the son and daughter of Andrew Baxter another old Fittie family has departed from the Squares.

Apart from the old order changing, some ominous developments were taking place in the 1970s. The village was becoming more isolated. 'There used to be five small shops in the Squares and another on Pocra Quay,' John Gillanders recalled. The surrounding traditional, labour intensive industries that had provided work for so long were begining to close down. At the same time those sectors of the oil-related industry that required considerable wharfage and storage space were creeping nearer. A dire warning came from across

John Gillanders. Born in 1908, he is one of Fittie's oldest residents, yet still an 'incomer' from Links Street. Photograph by former harbour pilot, Bill Clark.

the water. In 1971, on the eve of their restoration, 140 fisher cottages in Old Torry were made the subject of a compulsory purchase order and razed to the ground to provide land for an oil base. It was generally agreed that conservation measures had come to the Fittie Squares in the nick of time.

In recent years however, the area has had a welcome injection of new blood with doctors, oilmen, an artist, a sculptor and others with no harbour connections coming to live there. Their arrival can perhaps in part be attributed to the conservation measures, and they enjoy the feeling of seclusion, the sea air, and the fact that their homes are not part of some prestige estate of kit houses. It is a different sort of community from that of the close-knit fisherfolk, consisting of people who have chosen to live there, who have paid a sizeable sum for their homes and who are determined to preserve the amenity of what is admittedly a 'fragile' area.

There was an heartening example of the whole community, both new and traditional, pulling together in 1992. Since the early 1970s, Pocra Quay has housed mud silos, huge Martian structures which contain 'mud' or drilling fluid, chemical emulsions used in the oil industry to assist the drilling process. The mud company MGIT (Great Britain), based at Pocra where the cooperage had once stood, lodged a planning application for fifteen new silos some of which would be 50ft high. The site selected was just behind the firm's office which backs round to the north end of New Pier Road, where the 'Martian invaders' would be nicely placed to dominate the village. This application was seen as the thin end of the wedge. A meeting of residents packed the Mission Hall and unanimously opposed the application. Planning permission was subsequently refused and the silos had to go elsewhere. Indeed there was even talk of relocating some of those already *in situ*. Ruby Webster, in the front rank of the objectors, was delighted to see so many younger residents determined to preserve the heritage of the Squares. The episode showed too that lessons had been learned since the days of the Old Torry clearance which is now regarded as a panic decision.

Aberdonians continue to derive pleasure from walking through the Squares. There is a sense of pride about the place. Little gardens are scattered here and there, and artefacts symbolising the village's connection with the sea, lifebelts, buoys, shells and model ships decorate homes and gardens. But there is nothing of the *bijou* here, the area retains its character. Most heartening of all, there, seem to be more children playing in the Squares nowadays. There remains, however, for the outsider a very slight feeling of unease. It's a splendid place but it remains a private place.

Part Two

Education

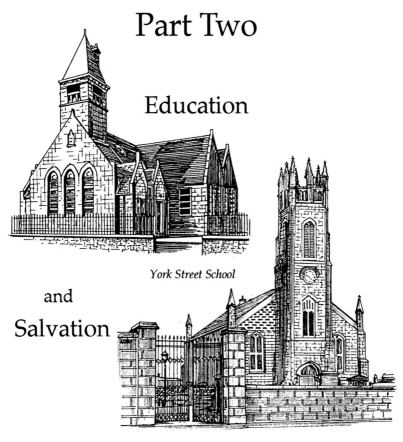

York Street School

and
Salvation

St Clement's Church

Chapter 5

The Schools of Footdee and St Clement's

Go down to the Fisher Square and lay hold of some little fellow hardly able to waddle about without assistance in his thick made-down moleskins, and you will find he has the Shorter Catechism at his tongue-end.

Quoted in Peter Anson's 'Fisher Boats and Fisher Folk', 1930

St Clement Street School which used to stand opposite St Clement's Kirk in what is now the Seaforth Maritime yard had a pedigree that went back over three hundred years. 'A school for instructing children in reading, writing and in the principles of arithmetic, was at an early period after the institution of the church, established at Futtie', wrote Kennedy in 1818. 'The institution of the church' to which he refers was the post-Reformation reopening of St Clement's Chapel as an Established Kirk in 1631. According to the book of Aberdeen Mortifications published in 1849, the parent Kirk Session of St Nicholas appointed the teacher, paid him his salary, sent poor scholars to be taught, occasionally furnished books, paid for fuel and even made the odd visit. Later the Session and magistrates appointed the dominie jointly while the Session continued to pay the salary. In the early days this 'did not exceed £2 15s 6d but was afterwards augmented by the Session till it amounted to £15 a year'.

The first schoolmaster we hear of, recalled in Ann Allardyce's memoir of the 1780s, is the dull and diligent Mr Robb whose cocked hat and long-skirted coat must have rendered him an alien figure amid the broad-bonneted, blue-jacketed fishermen:

He taught reading by the usual routine of going through the Shorter Catechism, Proverbs and Bible; he also gave instruction in writing and arithmetic, but his pupils seldom remained so long as to make any proficiency; nothing was explained to them and I believe no one would have presumed to ask a question.

A new dominie, Mr William Smith who was also session clerk of St Nicholas Church was appointed in 1791. The school at that time was near the Kirk, on the west side of Garvock Wynd as shown in Colin Innes's Plan of Footdee of 1803. In 1807 the quarterly fees, which had not gone up since 1779 were raised to Reading 3/6, Writing 2/6 and the two combined, 4/6 while Arithmetic and Writing were 5/-. Church Music at 1/-would have been taught by the deputy master who was also precentor at St Clement's. Parents presumably chose the 'modules' they could afford.

It is probably the same Mr Smith who is still there in 1828 when St Nicholas was disjoined and six new kirk sessions created. Smith was appointed clerk to them all on condition that he resign as master at Footdee School and there is the merest indication that he went with reluctance. The Town Council now took over the running of the school and with what seems an almost modern degree of bureaucracy 'remitted to the standing committee to consider and arrange a plan for procuring a successor, and to fix the amount of perquisites to be paid for the duties of said office'. After this great sayaway, the perquisites seem to have amounted to little more than fees paid by the scholars which in view of the poor area and sparse attendance must have been small indeed. In 1837 we find George Bruce, 'Teacher of St Clement's or Footdee School' requesting the magistrates for the security of a yearly salary. Since a salary had been paid by their predecessors, the Session of St Nicholas, one might have thought Bruce had a reasonable case. But his request was denied. The Council 'will not interfere, no Salary ever having been paid by the Council to the teacher of St Clement's School'. There are other indications that local teachers lived on the poverty line. To supplement what was doubtless a meagre salary, Mr Robb back in the 1780s, gave the young Ann Allardyce two hours private tuition in his usual 'dry and unvarying manner' and there were no regrets when she grew old enough to walk into Aberdeen for her schooling. In 1795 the Footdee Society records a loan of £2 to one of its members, the schoolmaster Lewis Middleton, a name usually associated with whaling. Whether he was dominie at Fittie or not it is impossible to say for this would appear to have been during the Smith era. The request of a loan was an unusual occurrence for the Society, but it was repaid with interest.

To give them their due, the Town Council, on taking over in 1832 did erect a new Footdee School somewhere near Waterloo Quay, but they allowed it an existence of scarcely thirty years. The Street Directory for 1861-62 notes a St Clement's School, also known as the Footdee Public School with fees of 3/6 to 7/6 a quarter. By that latter year of 1862, however it had vanished. In the late 1850s the Great North of Scotland Railway had carried its line from Kittybrewster to the old Canal Basin at Waterloo Quay and the terminus was now extended east as far as Church Street. Required now for railway development, the school site was sold by the Town to the GNSR for £600 and demolished at the very time when Footdee's population was increasing rapidly. In 1862, 1865, and again in 1867 and probably on other occasions during the 1860s Fittie folk, St Clement's Kirk Session, indeed 'all the influential people about the Quay' petitioned the magistrates for a school, arguing in 1865 that as 'a palace has been erected at the West-end for teaching boys of the well-to-do class (the new Aberdeen Grammar School building of 1863) something surely ought to be done for the handicraftsmen of the East-end'. They ask that the School be rebuilt on a larger scale and 'on a site nearly opposite St Clement's Church'.

In an article on 'Education in the Footdee District' published on November 8, 1865 the *Aberdeen Journal* gave its opinion. Defining the limits of the district as from the railway to the Bannermill 'there are about 2000 mechanics employed in Footdee' which with their dependants gives a very populous area'. The article then proceeds:

> The £600 as well as the materials of the old school which are stored up somewhere the Council must and will give. The Harbour Board should at least give the site, and might perhaps do a little more. The memorialists (petitioners) themselves, however, will need to come down liberally, so that a really first-rate school may be got.

As for the curriculum, 'the arts of navigation and mechanical drawing should be taught both during the day and in the evening - a great boon to such a population'. Nor are the girls forgotten:

> There would no doubt be adequate provision made for an efficent girls' department, where a truly useful education would be imparted and we see no reason why the art of cookery might not be turned to some practical account, and some provision made for giving a warm meal, at a cheap rate, to workmen at a distance from home.

Finally the paper warned, 'We think it will be in every way more advisable not to expect too much from the Council'.

Far from gifting the site, the Harbour Comissioners sold it in 1868, stipulating that the materials of the former school which belonged to them should be used in its erection. After a ten year hiatus the trustees of the new Footdee Public School announced its opening on Monday August 8, 1870 at Twelve o'clock Noon on the site desired by the petitioners on the St Clement Street/Church Street corner opposite the kirk, with the infant class under the charge of Miss Knowles, and the Juvenile and Senior Classes under Mr John McLauchlan. Senior work would include Navigation and Geometry, and classes were offered 'for Latin, French and Mathematics'. Fees were from 2d to 4d weekly. Evening classes would be available during the winter months. There were places for 300, but three years later the school was attempting to educate over 600 scholars.

Only three years later another, major change came about. The newly established Aberdeen School Board was willing to accept transfer of Footdee Public School to its own management - the acquisiton of schools of reasonable standard run by reputable bodies was part of the Board's remit - though the handover was initially delayed by the Harbour Commissioners who thought this would be an appropriate time to raise the feu duty. Aberdeen School Board inevitably had a low opinion of the premises it acquired from other bodies and pronounced Footdee School 'an inferior one-storey building'. They rebuilt on the same site and in March 1906 threw open for inspection their new, 'comfortable and cheerful' St Clement Street School, a neat building of granite ashlar designed by the Board architect, J A Ogg Allan. It was roof lit and the main hall was carried up through the height of the school. A gallery ran round the first floor. Plaster work was by the renowned firm of Bannochie. The school was enlarged in 1885 and by the turn of the century was educating children from Fish, Cotton, Miller, Prince Regent, and Baltic Streets in Upper Fittie, from St Clement Street, Waterloo Quay, Clarence Street and, the Fisher Squares.

Davidson's Schoolie was plain in appearance and vocational in outlook

York Street School had its origins in Davidson's School. In 1803, John Davidson, an Aberdeen goldsmith saved from drowning by two Fittie fishermen bequeathed £1000 in gratitude to establish a school 'for the free education of the children of White Fishers and Pilots....in and near to Footdee, containing two apartments, one for Girls, and another for Boys'. Pencilled in on Colin Innes Plan of 1803 at the Links end of York Place, Davidson's Schoolie was plain in appearance and vocational in outlook. The boys had Navigation and Book-keeping on their currriculum in addition to the three Rs while the girls were taught reading, writing, spinning, sewing and knitting. One estimable dominie was Alexander Brownie who during the mid-nineteenth century taught boys who later 'did exceptionally well and commanded the big ocean-going ships'. His opposite number was Miss Margaret Anderson. By 1874 Jane B Spalding and John McInnes were in charge, but subsequently Miss Spalding became sole teacher.

Thanks to Davidson's School, the scholars of the Fisher Squares were not deprived of education during the 'hiatus' of Footdee Public School, but Davidson's was bedevilled with overcrowding. Aberdeen School Board now came to the rescue, and not only 'resolved on its acquisition' but in 1881, true to form, built a new school a stone's throw to the west in York Street, resembling nothing so much as a stockily built church. A tablet on the school facade reads: *York Street School, 1881* but according to the Aberdeen Street Directory it remained as Davidson's for another decade, becoming York Street School only in 1891.

Miss Spalding remained at the helm, retiring eventually in 1905. Unfortunately the early logs and with them her comments have not survived though the vivid memories of this tall, immaculate and formidable woman remained with her pupils throughout their lives. She particularly disapproved of the common practice of keeping girls from school one day a week to help with the family wash. 'Oh that Footdee,' she would say when listening to some dubious excuse for non-attendance, 'it will go down like Sodom and Gomorrah for the lies that have been told.' My grandmother had been a pupil of Miss

York Street School

59

Spalding's, and some of her *bons mots* are among my earliest memories.

In 1837 John Smith had intended that the 'gap site' on the west side of North Square be used for housing at some point, just as in South Square. North Square, however, evolved differently for soon after the Disruption of 1843 St Clement's Free Church built its own school on the site. Miss Howling was mistress here during the 1860s, perhaps a daughter of the master of the ill-fated *Duke of Sutherland.* This Free Church School was subsequently demolished in 1870 to create space for three futher houses as already recounted. There is mention of a Free Church School planned for New Pier Road, or schooling could possibly have continued in the new North Square Mission Hall which was requested, it will be recalled, for general as well as religious purposes and is still known as 'The Schoolie'.

From March 1876, Free Kirk and other local children from Upper Fittie could attend Commerce Street School. Designed by Duncan McMillan in the style of an elegant country house with ecclesiastical overtones, it was opened with considerable ceremony as befitted Aberdeen School Board's first original school with the Lord Provost and magistrates in attendance and Dr Spence of the Free Kirk leading the prayers. During the first year the school log reported out-of-doors activities official and unofficial; 'Specimens are being collected for the School Museum; 'Attendance very irregular due to Aberdeen Races on Wed. and Thurs.' - at the nearby Links. By 1883 classes were being rearranged to cope with overcrowding. Commerce (locally pronounced Khmerse) Street School is the oldest of an architecturally outstanding trio of Board Schools that served the St Clement's area. Round the corner from Commerce Street looms Hanover Street School while Frederick Street School is glimpsed on the other side of the Beach Boulevard.

Hanover Street School had its origins in the North Parish Church's Albion Street School which originally stood on its site. It too was taken over by the Aberdeen School Board in 1879. Albion Street, once known as the Bool Road, long had a reputation as a 'hotbed of vice' and in 1894, and no doubt for that reason, the school was renamed Hanover Street which it also conveniently fronted. Three years later the image was further improved when a formidably handsome new school, designed by the distinguished architect Arthur Clyne rose on the site, foreshadowing the 1930s in style. It cost £11,000 and though built to accomodate over 650 pupils, the roll later rose to 1000. The old admission registers show no clear demarcation between Commerce Street and Albion/Hanover Street Schools, both drawing scholars from the same Upper Fittie streets, indeed from the same tenements.

Across the Beach Boulevard which eventually replaced Albion Street, the turretted Moorish palace of Frederick Street School had its origins in 1835 as Dr Bell's School, sharing with Old Aberdeen a £1000 endowment from Dr

The former Commerce Street School, left with Hanover Street School right, from the Tarry Briggie.

Andrew Bell of Madras. The initial roll consisted of 400 boys and 300 girls. English, Reading Grammar, Geography, History, Writing, Dictation, Arithmetic, Maths, Music and Drawing were taught and girls could take plain needle work and knitting in addition. In 1869 the classrooms were described as 'commodious and well-aired'. Dr Bell's was intended 'chiefly for the children of the working classes' and the fees at a maximum of 2d weekly attracted scholars from the Footdee, Shorelands and Gallowgate areas and even as far afield as Berryden, Hardweird in Gilcomston and Dee Village and Union Glen in Ferryhill.

Dr Bell's was taken over by Aberdeen School Board in 1878. Over the next few years, however, there were problems with discipline, and it was noted that 'the scholars are desitiute of books'. The building was becoming increasingly dingy and overcrowded, and by 1892 'something (was) very seriously wrong from a sanitary point of view'. Nevertheless Her Majesty's Inspector could still report a few year's later that 'though recruited from a poor locality, the entire school is marked by good bearing and a courteous tone'. A new school building was clearly a priority and the new Frederick Street School opened on the same site in 1905 at a cost of £18,000 with an amazing roll of 1096.

What was the fate of these five schools? St Clement Street, with its pedigree reaching back to the early 1630s later served as a primary school. Mrs

61

Ethel Kilgour of Links Street had her early schooling there, though her brother attended York Street, which was used as an overflow primary because of the enormous numbers of children in the area. She gives an account of her school days there in her memoir *A Time of our Lives.* 'At the sound of the handbell we would line up to troop back inside, some of the older pupils singing "come in an' get kilt, come in an' get kilt" to the considerable annoyance of the bell ringer usually a teacher named Miss Taylor'.

York Street having served as a primary became a nursery school in 1942, originally taking pupils from the Squares and Neptune Terrace as well as those from harbour families, from North Pier Villa on Pocra Quay, for example and Dock Gate House, York Place. In 1947 the log records that the air raid shelters were removed but the children were unable to go out to play because of the number of bricks lying around. On a cheerier note, the pupils go to the beach after lunch for the end of term picnic in July 1952.

With the number of children in the area sharply declining in the post-war years, York Street Nursery with forty places was opened to children from all over Aberdeen on a waiting list basis. And though its exterior still bears grime from Fittie's numerous lums, and the school itself seems almost engulfed by a neighbouring road transport firm, the interior has been attractively refurbished and an award has been won for the excellence of its work. In 1992 however, in the midst of considerable controversy the roll was cut down to twenty because it no longer served 'a community cachment area'.

Commerce Street School became redundant after the great slum clearances in the area and in the post-war era served as the Nursery Department for Hanover Street School, and as the Schools' Eye Clinic. Having been a store for some time, it was acquired by Format Communication Art and superbly refurbished in 1990 although looking slightly dockit without its handsome chimney pots. Hanover Street School alone continues as a primary and in recent years the roll has been around the 200 mark. Attempts to close it in the early 1980s were resisted. It is here that the children of Footdee come, though only a dozen or so compared with the hundreds of yore.

Frederick Street School subsequently became an Intermediate and then a Junior Secondary. 'Discipline was strong,' Ethel Kilgour recalls of the mid-thirties, 'but we had marvellous teachers.' She especially remembers her favourite teacher, Miss Cook who taught English. The quality of education is endorsed by Albert Elrick of Cotton Street who later won a bursary to the Central School while his brother George, also a pupil at Frederick Street, became a bursar at Robert Gordon's College. George Elrick is still well remembered as the presenter of 'Housewives' Choice on BBC Radio. Both boys unfortunately had to contend with the snobbery of their uptown classmates. After closure Frederick Street was refurbished by Grampian Region into twenty -seven 'starter units' and began a new lease of life in 1982 for those starting up in business.

In the 1960s, Footdee enjoyed an educational Indian summer when the new Aberdeen Commercial College with the dynamic Bernard Edwards at the helm, and as yet of no fixed abode, operated from St Clement Street, Commerce Street and Frederick Street Schools, and the church halls of East and West St Clements. The former was still functioning as a *bona fide* church hall which led on one memorable occasion to a class being taken in the graveyard when the ladies of the church, who were not involved with timetables, were making preparations for a Sale of Work. Staff and students alike grew to enjoy the peripatetic structure of the College and a great deal of time could be taken up in going from one venue to the next. The headquarters were at St Clement Street School and the old building would reverbate to the sound of a hundred typewriters. At lunchtime the College disbanded five minutes before Hall Russells down the road so that the buses could cope. St Clement's Street School was demolished in the 1970s. All is silence now.

The site of St Clement's School from Church Street, now a car park. Note St Clement's Church in the background. Today the barrier is the sole reminder of the school.

Chapter 6

Kirks and Missions

St Clement's Chapel, Futtie was originally founded by the magistrates and town council about the year 1498 for the devotional rites of the white fishers of Futtie, according to the rites of the Romish Church.

William Kennedy: Annals of Aberdeen 1818

There is a legend that in time immemorial a chapel was consecrated in Footdee to St Fotin who thus gave his name to the area. We can but speculate. The tale of the martyrdom of this nobly born nonagenarian Bishop of Lyons at the hands of the Romans during the second century is told in the *Aberdeen Breviary* which Bishop Elphinstone had printed in 1510. According to the *Breviary*, a Fotin cult subsequently spread throughout the world and particularly to the northern parts of Britain (the Latin of the original is vague here) especially the beach of the same (where) not far from sight of the River Dee a chapel was constructed in his honour. That is the clue for surmising it was sited in Fittie, although the candidacy of Torry which is rather nearer the Dee cannot be overlooked. Whatever the location of Fotin's 'basilica', allegiance was subsequently transferred to Clement and a chapel dedicated to him was founded well before the fifteenth century. It was a sort of pre-Reformation Chapel of Ease for the fishing community under the jurisdiction of St Nicholas Church, and possibly built on the same site as Fotin's shadowy chapel which would already have been consecrated ground.

Perhaps the earliest reference to St Clement's in the Council Registers, *pace* Kennedy, comes in 1467 when the heather thatch required repair. The Council Register makes reference to thirty-two 'thraw (twists) of thak hathir to Sanct Clementis kirk....' The priest at that time was Sir Ingram Bannerman (priests were commonly addressed as Sir) and he sought assistance from John Henrysoun the pynour (shoreporter). In 1498 funds were needed for the upkeep, probably not for the first and certainly not for the last time. The Council Register noted that the 'quhit fisheris (whitefishers) of Futy' pledged of their own free will to pay 'yerlie ilkan yer to Sanct Clementis chapel werk in Futy', 2/- from each master of a boat with two lines and twelve pence from 'ilkan botisman'. In 1510 and 1528, further sums were pledged for the support of the priests Sir Thomas Connyngton and Sir Alexander Russell. In the latter year 'maisteris, skiperis and servandis' (crew) were to pay 12 pence annually for the celebration of mass on Sunday and Friday. They did not, perhaps could not maintain these payments, and the Fittie Chapel, ignored, unendowed and ruinous long before the Reformation reached Aberdeen in 1560 was that year granted to Patrick Menzies for some unspecified secular use, provided he kept it 'wattertecht'. With no kirk of their own, Fittie folk showed a reluctance to trachle up to the Mither Kirk of St Nicholas as instructed, and so in 1600 a scale of fines was laid down for various forms of Sabbath breaking; forty pennies for non-attendance at St Nicholas, twenty shillings for selling fish (thair sall be na fische sauld, nor na mercatt of fisches) and forty shillings for fishing on the Sabbath.

By 1631, however, there were stirrings of conscience about the neglect of the Fittie folk's spiritual welfare. The excuse given in the Council Register is that the town's ministers already had enough problems on their hands:

> The inhabitantis of the toune of Futtie hes not bene cairfullie instructed in faithe and religion in tyme past, be resone of the great burdeine the ordinar pastors of the burgh does daylie undergoe.

Over fifty notable citizens now put their hands in their pockets and subscribed to fund a minister; among them Gilbert Menzies of Pitfodels who gave 'twa hundreth pundis', the controversial Dr William Guild, 'ane hundreth pundis' the same amount from Dr Patrick Dun Principal of Marischal College, 'three scoir pundis' from the renowned portrait painter George Jamesone while the newly appointed minister Mr Alexander Rosse chipped in with £60 13s 4d, all Scots. All told £4000 Scots (£200 sterling) was contributed. 'The ancient chapel,' according to Kennedy, 'was soon afterwards .....fitted up as a place of worship under the established church' and the graveyard, at that time containing many old tombstones was enclosed by a boundary dyke.

To secure further revenue, a glebe was created in 1633 when Bailie Thomas Gray, Burgess Andrew Meldrum and his wife Bessie Cay mortified four rigs of land adjacent to the kirk. St Clement's was officially re-established within the Church of Scotland by Act in Council in 1637. Fittie's ministers lived in interesting times. The Rev William Robertson signed the Covenant in 1638 and later found it advisable to flee the city, while the Rev Alexander Gray was deposed in 1716 after praying for the Pretender. Money remained a problem. The covenanting Robertson had once unsuccessfully contested the parish of Rayne probably because it had 'ane fine Stipend'· and his successors at St Clement's found it necessary to do some upmarket moonlighting. Robert Downie, minister from 1652 until 1666 was the first City Librarian and organised the 'flitting' of the city library from St Nicholas Kirk to Marischal College. He also found time to publish several volumes of poetry. The Rev George Abercrombie (1745-59) was the first headmaster of Robert Gordon's Hospital while to keep the honours more or less even, the Rev Alexander Fullerton (1774-87) was a master at the Grammar School.

The ancient chapel was still in use. In 1785 its ruinous state was brought to the attention of the Town Council and plans were put forward for a new church with a belfry, a gallery at each end and seating for up to 600 worshippers. Bailie John Copland offered to finance the building of the kirk and the Council gratefully accepted his scheme. It would cost him £400 but he would recoup his outlay over a period of twenty-one years on the seat rents, 'save for the poor fishers of Fittie who are free', on glebe rents and revenue from mortifications. We are now in the era described by Ann Allardyce and it is clear that there were at this time enough residents in the village, doubtless including those in the tiled houses, who could afford to pay seat rents and make the speculation worth Bailie Copland's while. The ancient chapel was finally taken down. Copland's Kirk was completed by 1787 and is shown in Milne's Plan adjacent to the west wall. According to Joseph Robertson it was 'more than once enlarged' which would help to swell Copland's seat rents. The bailie is said to have done well out of the arrangement, so much so that when it expired in 1808, the then minister, the legendary Rev John Thomson petitioned the Council that this revenue now be paid 'to the Incumbent and his Successors' and it was not until after his death in 1837 that the Council resumed the payment of fixed stipends.

Parson Gordon in his *Description* of 1661 states that 'it is a paroshen by it self and hes its ain parosh church', but as already noted, St Clement's was a 'branch' of the city parish church of St Nicholas. In 1828, however, St Nicholas was disjoined and St Clement's became one of Aberdeen's six new fully fledged *quoad civilia* parishes. It was appropriate that the new parish have a church both to match its premier division status and to accommodate its expanding congregation, and the building we see today, one of John Smith's handsome pinnacled triplets, was erected on the same site in 1828 at a cost of £2,500. (The others are the Kirk o Nigg, 1828, and the former South Parish Church,1830, in Belmont Street). 'It is a neat building', Robertson wrote of the new St Clement's, 'in the Gothic style, with an elegant tower or belfry'.

Having made do with a chapel that must have been in a tumbledown state for much of its three hundred years, Fittie folk were now treated to two new churches almost within forty years, and both during the fifty year ministry of the Rev John Thomson MD. He was one of the most remarkable men to minister in Footdee. A little, thin man with a distinct personality', Gammie describes him in *The Churches of Aberdeen* (1909) and a surviving portrait shows a hint of the manic. Doctor and minister both, he was a pillar of strength to the fishers, tending their bodies as well as their souls. He doubtless eased their inevitable worries at the time of the removal to the Sandness. Thomson and his opposite number at the Kirk o Nigg, the equally renowned Dr Cruden corresponded and each assisted the other at the sacrament of Communion when there were huge attendances. Thomson, of whom numerous anecdotes survive, paid a generous £5 4s 7d as his membership subscription to the Footdee Society and bequeathed what money he had to the poor of the parish.

He was succeeded in 1838 by his assistant the Rev Alexander Spence. Momentous times lay ahead. In 1843 a long-runing dispute within the Church of Scotland over the right of a laird or patron to appoint a minister came to a head. This right was unacceptable to many adherents, and at a historic meeting of the General Assembly that May, the Disruption of the Church of Scotland took place. Over a third of the ministers and many congregations 'came out', that is they left the Established Church to set up the Free Kirk. In Aberdeen city, although the patron, the Town Council, did not interfere in the choice of ministers, nevertheless all fifteen city ministers 'came out' as a matter of principle. Dr Spence had attended the fateful meeting in Edinburgh, and by the time he returned to Footdee, most of his congregation had, in a pre-emptive strike, erected Aberdeen's first Free Church, a wooden kirkie on the corner of Baltic Street. Descendants of these first Free Kirkers still recall tales of how their forebears worked through the night to get the roof on. The building was completed, an interdict forestalled, and Dr Spence preached there 'to a great congregation' on June 4 1843, the first Sunday of the Free Kirk's existence.

A unique Disruption Scroll of February 1843 survives and is printed in the booklet *St Clement's Parish Aberdeen* (1989) by Rosemary A Baxter. It contains the signatures or marks of nearly a thousand adherents, indicating their readiness to leave the Established Church and includes the names of well known shipbuilding and seafaring families: William Simpson and Grace Simpson; Alexander Hall and E (Elizabeth presumably) Hall of York Street; the Vernon family of York Place; an employee of Vernon & Co; the Howlings and Ligertwoods; numerous families from the Squares, the Quays, the Pottery and all the Footdee streets, many of them long gone now, as far west as Commerce Street and Virginia Street. There are signatures too from further afield, Broad Street, Gallowgate, Castle Hill, Shiprow, Adelphi.

Those who remained loyal to the Established Kirk soldiered on, 'leaving no word of bitterness' in the Kirk Session records. They experienced mixed fortunes. Just prior to the Disruption, Provost Thomas Blaikie presented a handsome gasolier, a redundant chandelier from St Nicholas Church converted for gas, and benefactions continued when the shipbuilder William Duthie, 'a hearty giver during his life' bequeathed £1000 to the Church Meal and Coal fund in 1869. His brother John gifted the organ in 1875. On the debit side, in 1848 the church lost the great part of its poor funds, including the Rev Thomson's Bequest when the Leys Masson mill at Grandholm collapsed. Provost Leys and his partner and brother-in-law Provost Brebner owned land and ran businesses in Fittie which had perhaps prompted the Session to invest their funds in the Woodside firm. The following year the Rev James Newlands who had replaced Dr Spence and subsequently taken to drink was deposed, doubtless an embarrassment to his son, the dominie at Davidson's School. Good men followed however, the Rev James Fraser and the Rev G F I Philip, and in 1879 that St Clement's had in the Rev. Charles Cadell Macdonald a minister of outstanding calibre. He was a notable orator who spoke his mind freely, played golf on the Links and had 2000 adults in his congregation. It was during C C's era that the great fund-raising three day Bazaars were organised by the ladies of the congregation, and which according to the Rev A C Dow 'brought forth a response from Futtie which was noticeably lacking in the Sunday collections'. However, Gammie writing about St Clement's in 1909 when C C still had over ten years to serve strikes an elegiac and prophetic note:

The district of Footdee is not what it once was. The revolution of its industries, the migration of the population to other parts of the city have told severely; and what has affected the district has affected the church. Its membership is still large, but it is no

Rev Dr C C Macdonald

longer in the same sense the church of a resident population. The members are scattered all over the city, and their connection perhaps in too many cases is largely a nominal one. To this fact also may be attributed the unsatisfactory attendances at the ordinary diets of worship....We are far from the days when the Church of St Clement's was in the heart of a community of its own.

We now turn to follow the adventures of the Free Kirkers, who back in 1843, had in a matter of months, moved from their wooden kirk in Baltic Street to a new stone church nearby in Prince Regent Street. Like the wooden kirkie it was filled to overflowing and was replaced in turn in 1883 by a large and

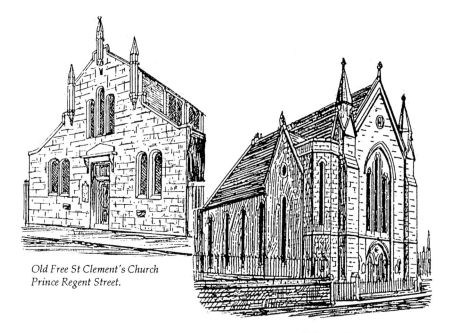

Old Free St Clement's Church
Prince Regent Street.

St Clement's Free
(West St Clement's Church)

handsome Gothic church by the distinguished architect A. Marshall Mackenzie. It was sited on the corner of Fish Street, just below Commerce Street
School. (As a matter of interest, the superfluous Prince Regent Street building
was first acquired for the use of Gaelic-speaking fishermen then was rented by
the Salvation Army. From 1889 it housed St Clement's Episcopal Mission with
the remarkable and much loved Rev John Comper as the guiding spirit.
Comper, whose son Ninian was to become the leading church architect of his
day, left 'the congenial congregation' of St John's Episcopal Church to establish St Margaret's in the Gallowgate. When it, as he said, had become 'almost
too respectable' he set out to minister to the poor of the quays and harbour area
from the Prince Regent Street church, now St Clement's Episcopal. The church
later moved to Regent Quay and became St Clement's-on-the-Quay, where the
service, in spite of the humble surroundings followed High Church rites. St
Clement's subsequently flitted to Mastrick. As for the Prince Regent Street
building, some older Fittie folk recall it ending its days as the Plaza Ballroom).

Dr Spence of St Clement's Free died in 1890, the last survivor of Aberdeen's Disruption ministers. In 1900, following the union of the Free Church
with the United Presbyterian Church, the kirk became St Clement's United
Free. It was said at this time that 'everybody who was anybody in Footdee was

70

connected with St Clement's UF ' and for an east end kirk, there was a remarkable number of city and harbour personalities in the flock including the Lord Provost Sir Alexander Lyon. The church's popularity can be attributed in great measure to the Rev A D Donaldson, a worthy succesor to Dr Spence. In spite of the trend of the population westwards, Gammie noted: 'it is no small tribute to minister and people to say that the membership which was 578 at the time of Mr Donaldson's settlement in 1878 is now over 700', adding that he and C C had frequently exchanged pulpits.

Rev A D Donaldson

In 1929 the Established and Free Kirks reunited and St Clement's Parish and St Clement's UF become respectively East and West St Clement's. After a ministry of fifty-two years at West St Clement's, the Rev. A D Donaldson was succeeded in 1930 by the Rev Victor Caldwell who was to serve until 1950. In the inter-war years there was much musical talent in the congregation and the hall was packed when a number of lively productions were staged under the direction of Miss Maggie Garden for many years the church's organist and choirmaster.

The Belles of the Village
Performed by St Clements United Free Church Choir

In 1963 with their congregations declining, the two charges united with East St Clement's, the original parish church becoming the chosen place of worship. The congregation of West St Clement's presented their central block of pews to symbolise the union. Their church was demolished in 1974 and the site is now covered with grass and trees. In 1985 the incumbent of the united charge resigned in difficult circumstances and in view of the kirk's decreasing roll Aberdeen Presbytery decided on dissolution in May 1987. As if to symbolise these sad times, St Clement's lost its coronet. Its distinctive pinnacles were declared unsafe and removed and the kirk that once was vibrant with the oratory of the Reverends Thomson, Spence, Macdonald and the visiting Donaldson stood dockit and forlorn, virtually overwhelmed by the surrounding demolition and industrialisation. To preserve the memory however, valued items from the kirk were gifted to the city by the congregation. In 1990 Aberdeen City Council resolved to restore St Clement's, though for a secular use as in 1560. Made 'wattertecht' by 1993, with pinnacles restored it is now destined to beome a repository for the city archives.

St Clement's Kirkyard in September 1992. A row of pinnacles await restoration to form the church's distinctive coronet.

Down at the Fisher Squares, two missions co-existed for a number of years. It all began in 1859 at Leith when a Captain Summers of Fraserburgh along with his crew experienced the religious revival then sweeping Scotland and became converted. Later, becalmed at Pocra they made good use of the time to hold revivalist meetings in the Free Kirk School in North Square.

' Even the rafters were occupied', wrote Andrew Baxter in his memoir *Bygone Days of Footdee:'* What an effect it had on the village. Men and women who were addicted to drink were converted; cursing and swearing were exchanged for prayer and hymn singing. The whole place became a veritable garden of the Lord'. Donald Ross the evangelist of the North-East Coast Mission, 'strict and rigid in doctrine, blunt and fearless in expression' was appointed superintendent at Footdee and drew such large crowds that in 1869 Fittie folk successfully petitioned the Town Council's Links and Bents Committee for a site on which to erect 'a Building for Religious Meetings and General Purposes'. And so the present Mission Hall, the 'Schoolie' was built in the centre of North Square which had not followed the layout of South Square as originally anticipated and had no Middle Row. Originally the Mission represented a Free Kirk presence in the Squares, but the services were more evangelical in style. A bell to call the people to worship was presented by the Earl of Kintore which in more recent times was blown down during a storm. Apparently it has never sounded the same since it was repaired.

The Mission Hall

In the old days the 'Schoolie' would be packed and the Bible class was held in the gallery. Fittie folk at one time would attend both the 'Schoolie' on a Sunday as well as East or West St Clement's or perhaps the Gordon Mission in Justice Street. The 'Schoolie's' Wednedsay meetings were popular when 'a hymnie or two' would be sung, and they continue to draw a congregation from the Squares. The Mission was requisitioned during the war and £300 was subsequently awarded to cover renovation and redecoration. At the helm in those days was former skipper and local chronicler Andrew Baxter, a member of an old Fittie family which had been part of the Mission from its earliest days. He became superintendent in 1925 and after half-a-century of service died in 1977 at the age of 95, long-lived like many of his generation. His successor John 'Sonny' Stephen was superintendent from 1954 until retiring in 1991 at 77, although his links with the Mission, went back for over sixty years. Local folk and helpers now carry on the work of the Mission which is also used for meetings.

Donald Ross the first superintendent subsequently joined the Plymouth Brethern and with some converts from the Mission set up a branch of the Brethern in Footdee. Ross was to continue his evangelical trail-blazing career in America while David and Andrew Fowler took over Brethern work at Fittie. Their place of worship, the Walker Hall (the Hallie) was built in New Pier Road. A new Walker Hall, the Gospel Hall was built on the same site in 1951 but closed forty years later and was subsequently rented by the artist Joyce Cairns as a studio.

The Gospel Hall

Chapter 7

St Clement's Kirkyard and its Residents

One hundred merks to be imployit for the upholding of the dyik of the kirk zearde of Futtie....which I causit built.

Will of George Davidson of Pettens, 1633

Although the leafy kirkyard of St Clement's has been a burial ground for centuries, the six hundred and more memorials one sees there today date largely from the nineteenth century and are among the most interesting in Aberdeen. There are memorials to mariners who perished in all corners of the globe, to the shipmaster Robert Cattanach, for example, who died at Kingston, Jamaica in 1824 aged 38. His shipmaster sons William, who died in Laguna, South America in 1839 aged 29 and John, at the mouth of the Danube in 1847 aged 25 are commemorated on the same stone. There are memorials to those who perished at the bar of Aberdeen harbour such as the Essex-born Captain Edward Howling, master of the *Duke of Sutherland* which foundered at the North Pier in 1853. In the neighbouring grave lies his nephew Peter Ligertwood whose death was particularly poignant. The story of the tragedy is told in Chapter 10.

The great shipbuilders are remembered. We find the family vault of John Duthie, the coffin-like tomb of William Duthie 'merchant and shipowner in Aberdeen' and a memorial to that redoubtable Duthie-in-law Captain John Cargill who so memorably piloted the royal yacht *Victoria and Albert* to Waterloo Quay in September 1848. There are memorials to the Hall family including 'the burial place of Alexander Hall shipbuilder', ten of his children and two Wilson grandchildren. Here too are interred the great Footdee ministers, John Thomson MD and Charles Cadell Macdonald DD. There are memorials to a whole way of life in Fittie; to ship carpenters, pilots, mariners,

A group of memorials to members of the Hall family. The one surmounted by the urn commemorates Alexander Hall, his wife Elizabeth Cochar, and their sons James and William Hall and William's son Alexander who died in Nagasaki in 1876 aged 28. The tablet on the wall is in memory of Alexander Hall Morgan 'a native of Footdee - Shipbuilder in Whampoa, China.'

The cross in the foreground marks the resting place of the Rev Charles Cadell Macdonald while the tomb behind is in memory of William Duthie, merchant and shipowner.

engineers, ropemakers, fishermen, harbourmaster, trawlmaster, tidewaiter, fishcurer, blacksmith, iron founder, iron moulder, coastguard. The gravestone of Lauritz Rassmussen, stevedore, linguist, and a former pilot on the River Plate is handsome in the art nouveau style. Rassmussen seems to have led an exciting life before settling in Aberdeen. He served in the Brazilian Navy during the Paraguay War of 1866-72 and was captured and put in irons. He lived in Torry for a time, naming his house La Plata in memory of the old days, before crossing the water to live in the Neptune Terrace enclave off York Street.

Old tragedies are not forgotten. Here are the cousins John Tait Sim and Charles Sim, cook and apprentice, lost from the *Oscar* whaler 'of this place who was bound for the Greenland Fishery and was totaly *(sic)* wrecked on Grays Head (Greyhope) twixt this harbour and Girdleness' in 1813. George Liddle is remembered on his grandfather's gravestone. The seventeen-year-old lad was shipwrecked in 1864 when the *Invercauld*, launched that year from John Smith's yard on the Inches struck on Auckland Island south of New Zealand in a hurricane. Young George died of starvation ten weeks later. Of the crew of twenty-five, only three survived, including the first mate Andrew Smith, whose account of the tragedy, *The Castaways* was published in Aberdeen in 1866.

There are memorials to the Ogston dynasty, the founder of the line, the soap manufacturer Alexander Ogston, merchant, who died in 1838, also Soapy's grandson, Professor Sir Alexander Ogston (1844-1929), responsible for great advances in bacteriology and antiseptic surgery. (Soapy Ogston, like Jimmy Hay, Cocky Hunter and Raggy Morrison are names still affectionately recalled in Aberdeen though the memory of their actual owners has grown dim).

One memorial whose inscription is now obliterated is dedicated to 'Alexander Marr many years shipbuilder in Footdee' who died in 1830 at the age of ninety. He and his spouse left their estate to charity, including £100 to the poor of Footdee. The Operative Shipwright Friendly Society was destined to receive a legacy of £40 had it not 'predeceased' its benefactor. However, Marr's trustee, his fellow shipbuilder Alexander Hall arranged that the bequest fund the education at St Clement's School of four sons between eight and twelve years of age of local operative shipwrights 'in needful circumstances'. Serious scholars only need apply: 'These Boys shall know the Alphabet, and shall be able to read words of one or two syllables, and their Parents or Guardians shall supply them with Books....and shall cause them to be kept in a condition similar to their other school companions'.

At the east side of the kirk stands a slender obelisk at whose point is an anchor with the initial B slotted through, making it appear double. Is perhaps a leading member of the Boys' Brigade buried here? No, in fact the design was

The Brodie obelisk.

by the sculptor Alexander Brodie (1830-67) who died some sixteen years before the BB was founded. He erected the stone in memory of his father, a seaman, an older brother drowned at Quebec at the age of 27 and other members of the family. Born in Garvock Wynd, Brodie studied art thanks to the largesse of the philanthropist Sheriff Watson. Best known of his works are the statues of Queen Victoria now in the Town House vestibule, the peripatetic Priest Gordon currently to be found in the garden of St Peter's Primary School in King Street, and the bust of his friend the Gilcomston-born artist, John 'Spanish' Philip. Brodie committed suicide, unable it seems to cope with the pressures of fame and the number of commssions. The architect William Ramage (1820-66) lies below a memorial of square, simple, solid masonry erected by the freemasons of Aberdeen. Circular marks left on the tomb indicate the probable removal of masonic symbols by vandals. Ramage's work in Aberdeen includes Elmhill House at Cornhill, the former Militia Barracks in King Street now a bus depot and said to be haunted, his own home, a unique 'double cottage' in Waverley Place, and, with Archibald Simpson, the

The tomb of William Ramage.

Mechanics' Institue in Market Street, where he taught. It is now a hotel. Buried here too is the bookseller David Wyllie (1777-1844) who produced Aberdeen's first Street Directory in 1824, and whose bookshop in Union Street survived until the 1960s. On the outer wall of the kirk itself is a plaque in memory of a devoted member of the congregation, David Grant (1833-1893), a tobacconist to trade and an excellent amateur musician. It attributes to him the composition of the famous psalm tune, Crimond.

The kirkyard was enclosed by a dyke in 1637 soon after the re-establish-

The Crimond plaque.

79

ment of the church by the magistrates. Thirteen years later another dyke or wall, doubtless more substantial, was gifted. On the north wall an inscription carved on a sandstone tablet tells the tale: *George Davidson, elder, Burges of Abd bigit this dyk on his own expenses 1650*. Davidson, a sucessful packman or pedlar was the seventeenth century equivalent of a retail draper. As a notable benefactor to the city his standing locally would have been akin say to that of Lord Fraser of Allander in the twentieth century. He had been admitted a burgess of the city in 1626 and was one of those who subscribed to the reinstatement of St Clement's in 1631. His donation of £333 6s 8d Scots was one of the most generous. In the ensuing years he acquired the estates of Pettens in Belhelvie parish, then Westburn, Bogfairly and Kepplehills (now Newhills), before building the St Clement's dyke. He died in 1663 and his will makes a number of interesting mortifications including the Lands of Pettens and Bogfairly to the Town, 500 merks (a merk equalled 13/4 Scots) for the poor of Futtie, and '100 merks to be imployit for the upholding of the dyik of the kirk zearde (yard) of Futtie and the Bridge of Bogs burne (Bucksburn) which I causit built'. If the truth be told, however, the dyke we see today, encompassing the churchyard to the north and east, is not the one that Davidson built at his own expense in 1650, in spite of the plaque. It is much younger! Kennedy, in his *Annals* of 1818 discusses the demolition of the old chapel and the building of Copland's Kirk in 1787 and notes that 'the cemetery and the area

The George Davidson tablet. The coat of arms is thought to be spurious and the wall is of a later date.

in front of it was surrounded by a proper wall'. Davidson's dyke was presumably now showing its age in spite of the fact that funds had been provided for its upkeep. Kennedy adds in a revealing footnote: 'There was fixed in the old wall, and has been *rebuilt in the new* a stone bearing the following inscription...'and he goes on to quote the '*George Davidson...bigit this dyk*' legend noted above.

Apart from the wall which is 'B' listed, one other possible relic from Copland's Kirk of 1787 survives. The eastmost clock-face on the tower differs from the other two and is thought to have been transplanted from Copland's Kirk. It could well have been the work of Charles Lunan (1760-1816) a notable Aberdeen clock and watchmaker. Though not a resident of St Clement's Churchyard, Lunan's obituary in the *Edinburgh Evening Courant* of January 20 1816 is appropriate to a chapter such as this:

A man of uncommon shrewdness, intelligence and native strength of mind and from his inventive genuis in mechanics much might have been expected had his mechanic's mind received a more early culture, a circumstance which he often regretted during the latter part of his life. He has, however, left behind him many specimens of his ingenuity and of the accuracy with which he could execute the finest peices of mechanism.

The Lunan clock-face.

81

Although Davidson's tablet remains in excellent condition, and much work has been done towards the restoration of the church, the greater part of this unique graveyard, at least at time of writing, gives cause for concern. Those headstones in sandstone have weathered badly, and all are begrimed, victims of the polluted air of Fittie in its industrial heyday. Fortunately Sheila M Speirs compiled a painstaking guide to the memorials in 1988, and no visitor to the kirk should be without her booklet, *The Kirkyard of St Clement's (Aberdeen)* published in 1988 by the Aberdeen and North East Scotland Family History Society. Since then the stones have contined to weather and several are in the process of keeling over. The City Council maintain the kirkyard and the grass is carefully cut, but unfortunately the isolated position of St Clement's and its propinquity to Aberdeen's so-called red light district means that the graveyard attracts undesirables at night. This is one of the most ancient and hallowed places in Aberdeen, standing on the same site as the early mediaeval chapel to St Clement which in turn may have succeeded St Fotin's chapel. Moreover it is the resting place of many brave, talented and generous Aberdonians. The final stages of the restoration of the Church should hopefully include the reinstatement of the graveyard.

After the first edition of this book was published, Mr Stanley Rothney restored the headstones of George Liddle and another victim of the *Invercauld* disaster, Alexander Henderson, whose stone was erected by his brothers George and John Henderson, sailmakers.

The refurbishment of St Clement's Kirk, has been completed and at time of writing it still awaits a new role.

Part Three

The Quays and the Hinterland

The Round House

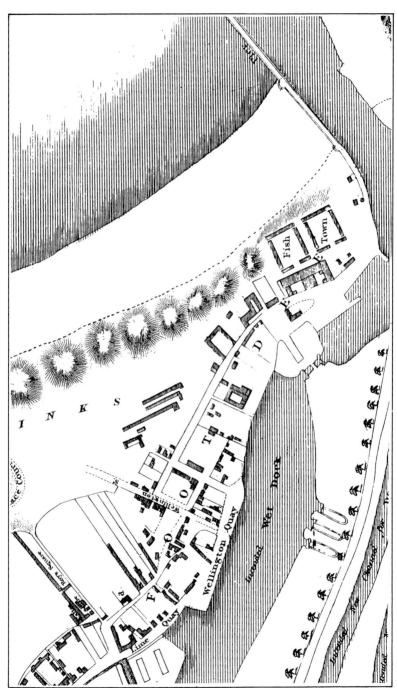

Wood's Plan, 1821, illustrates the definition of Footdee 'from Canal Basin (the shaded oblong, upper left, unmarked), to the New Pier', right. Note the channel linking the Canal Basin with the Wet Dock. Right of the Canal Basin is the Lime Quay with the Lime Basin below (unmarked), and 'Wellington' (Waterloo) Quay.

Chapter 8

Waterloo Quay

Footdee: from Canal Basin to New Pier.

Aberdeen Street Directory 1824 - 25

From Canal Basin to New Pier. Such is the definition of Footdee in the first street directory of 1824 and so it continues until the canal basin was infilled in 1855. As for the New Pier, it appeared as early as 1755. Kennedy wrote: 'About that time the Pocra pier was erected, and was long known by the name of the new pier'. For the modern reader attempting to locate Footdee, none of this is very helpful. What the directory is defining as Footdee - and its editor David Wyllie had Fittie connections and knew what he was talking about - was the area from the foot of Commerce Street to Pocra. Colin Innes's Plan of Footdee of 1803 follows Wyllie's description to the letter. The canal basin is shown as a large oblong on the left-hand side of the Plan, indicating the western boundary of Fittie, while the neat octagon of the Round House to the extreme right indicates the Pocra-North Pier extremity. As for the Fisher Squares at the Sandness, they were only fifteen years old when the first directory was issued and not important enough to merit enclosure.

The Aberdeen-Inverurie or Aberdeenshire Canal was rather older than Waterloo Quay and in Innes's Plan the basin sits in isolation. At that time the canal's existence was tenuous. It was first mooted in the early 1790s, but lack of investment and arguments about where exactly it should go delayed its opening until 1805 and that was for the transport of goods alone. The less cost-effective passenger service did not commence until 1807, and that was operated from Kittybrewster. Eleven locks were necessary to carry the canal

85

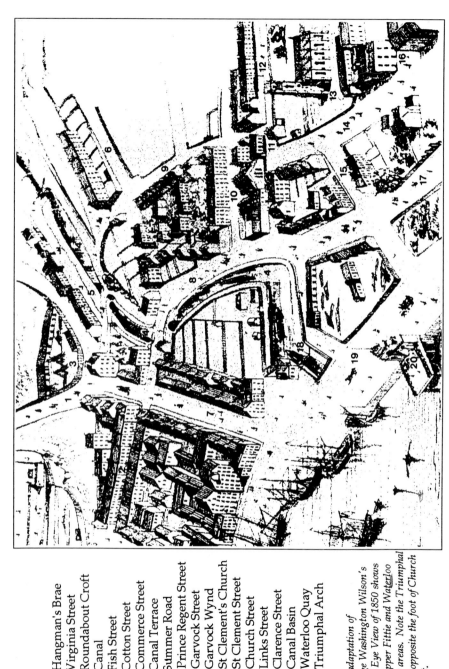

1 Hangman's Brae
2 Virginia Street
3 Roundabout Croft
4 Canal
5 Fish Street
6 Cotton Street
7 Commerce Street
8 Canal Terrace
9 Summer Road
10 Prince Regent Street
11 Garvock Street
12 Garvock Wynd
13 St Clement's Church
14 St Clement Street
15 Church Street
16 Links Street
17 Clarence Street
18 Canal Basin
19 Waterloo Quay
20 Triumphal Arch

This adaptation of George Washington Wilson's Birds Eye View of 1850 shows the Upper Fittie and Waterloo Quay areas. Note the Triumphal Arch opposite the foot of Church Street.

up to Kittybrewster which is said to have taken two days, slow even by early nineteenth century standards. Financial constraints also inhibited perhaps the principal *raison d'etre* of the project which had been urged by Thomas Telford in 1802, the forming of 'a proper connexion between the Canal and the Wet Docks'. For years goods were unloaded from incoming vessels then trundled or manhandled across the quay. A railway had been built in 1816 for this task, but there is doubt as to whether it was actually used. Eventually in 1834 a channel was constructed under Waterloo Quay and the long, low wooden barges could be manoeuvred into the dock for loading. Beside the basin was a cluster of warehouses including the 'Earl of Elgin's coalshed'. Doubtless the seventh Earl's dispatch of coal and lime from his Fifeshire mines and limeworkings, eventually to Inverurie via the Canal was a venture less controversial than his recent removal of sections of the Parthenon frieze for sale to the British Museum. The area around the canal was by no means industrialised, however, with gardens and a potato patch nearby.

During the first half of the nineteenth century the canal played a major role in Aberdeenshire's agricultural revolution and the scene around the Waterloo Quay basin must have been one of great activity with men loading the barges with lime, bones and dung for manuring the fields of the Inverurie hinterland, as well as with coals, and bricks and tiles for house-building. Carts would be standing by to take away the grain shipped in from the hinterland, over a thousand tons of it in 1831, and five years later over six thousand. In fact business boomed for the thirty regular barges during the canal's last twenty years when rates were halved. The transport of lime, loaded at the neighbouring Lime Basin and kept apart because of its deleterious nature, had, for example, risen from 2526 tons in 1831 to nearly 5000 tons in 1840. Nevertheless, the Aberdeenshire Canal had never been profitable for the Canal Company who in 1853 gratefully accepted an offer of £36,000 (it had cost £40,000)

Waterloo Station in its heyday. Note the steeple of St Clement's Kirk behind.

87

from the Great North of Scotland Railway (GNSR) who planned to lay a line between Aberdeen and Inverurie and points north alongside the canal bed, and in places actually in it. Indeed the purchase of the canal had not been confirmed by Parliament and lawyers were still wrangling over it when an impatient railway contractor breached the bank near Kintore, stranding a number of barges.

Two years later the GNSR's Waterloo Passenger and Goods Terminus was built on the basin and extended into Footdee as far as Church Street. Meanwhile, nearly a mile up the road at Guild Street, the Aberdeen Railway which served points south had established its terminus. Horse-drawn wagons were used to transport goods between the two stations, while mails were taken to Waterloo in a fast gig. If the south train were late however, passengers in transit further north had to run along the quays, sometimes to find the Waterloo gates shut in their faces. The GNSR was an avid timekeeper and the mails could not be delayed. Such a state of affairs could not be tolerated and in 1867, the GNSR and the Aberdeen Railway's successor, the Caledonian, established their Joint Station in Guild Street. Waterloo Terminus continued as the GNSR headquarters and as a busy goods station, ideally situated for handling freight shipped into Aberdeen harbour.

After being demoted to a single line goods station, however, Waterloo began a slow death. The passenger shelter rotted away and was removed in

The former GNSR goods shed near the site of the Canal Basin

the 1960s. Staff were relocated in the late 1970s, and a number of the stone buildings were demolished in 1986. In 1992, a delapidated Waterloo yard, though with its rails still intact, was offered for sale by BR. A number of commercial enterprises are now based there. Officially the former Waterloo Station is on Regent Quay, not Waterloo, but it seems to occupy a no man's land between the two, a throwback to its days as the canal basin. Around this dismal spot is what passes for Aberdeen's red light district, so a walk along Waterloo Quay particularly at night should be undertaken with caution. The bobbies, however, monitor the kerbcrawlers and the Fittie folk monitor the bobbies.

Waterloo Quay itself was begun when old Fittie village was cleared, or at least that part of it along the shore, and was completed by 1811. It was not named until after the great battle of 1815, however, and may prior to that have been briefly known as Wellington Quay. The North Pier was being extended at the same time so if heavy seas prevented work on the pier, John Gibb, Permanent Superintendent of Works kept his men busy on the new quay. Gibb's alternative title, Resident Harbour Engineer was carried out to the letter for between 1809 and 1816 he lived at Waterloo Quay, sometimes noted in the street directories simply as 'Footdee'.

The new quay would contain the future wet dock as recommended by Telford in 1802. Its construction, however, was delayed by rows between progressive and regressive factions, and by the city's bankruptcy between 1818 and 1825. By 1829, however, work started on its excavation and Waterloo and Regent Quays were joined. The Lime Quay which lay between the two seems to have continued in name for some years. In spite of the unpleasant nature of the product that was unloaded on its quayside, it had a little community of its own. John Duthie, hairdresser, had premises there and the office of the *Hazard*, the Hamburg packet, which sailed every six weeks was at Lime Quay as was the home of its master, Captain John Smith. The Aberdeen Lime Company was briefly based here until the late 1830s, when it 'flitted' to larger premises on Provost Blaikie's Quay on the Inches. The Lime Basin itself was transformed into a lagoon when Regent and Waterloo Quays were joined. It was infilled in 1835 and became the lower end of Church Street.

The Harbour Act of 1843 empowerd the newly created Harbour Commissioners to borrow £270,000 for further development. Work on the new wet dock, later to be called Victoria Dock, continued in earnest in 1846, and fortunately was just completed by September 7 1848 when no less a person than the Queen herself, en route for Balmoral, sailed in a day earlier than expected. The royal yacht, the wooden paddle steamer *Victoria and Albert* had been piloted from Woolwich at a great lick by Captain John Cargill, a brother-in-law of John Duthie of the renowned shipbuilding firm and master of the Aberdeen Steam Navigation Company's *City of London*. Cargill tied up at

The arrival of the Royal Party.

Waterloo Quay which was handy since he lived there. Opposite the foot of Church Street, a wooden jetty had been tricked out with fine crimson cloth, while in front of it a splendid triumphal arch painted to imitate granite, albeit with the scaffolding not yet removed, awaited the royal arrival. Local dignitaries were caught on the hop, and the *hoi polloi* hastened to Waterloo Quay where they appropriated positions reserved for their betters. Special constables were summoned to restore order. The royal party dutifully did not disembark officially until the following day, when they were greeted by the serried ranks of the Aberdeen Mafia, professors and ministers to the left, magistrates and militia on the right. To the fore was Provost George Thompson of the Aberdeen White Star Line, the silver keys of the city in his hand and his personal logo of twin white stars flanking the gilt lettering of 'Victoria' on the parapet. Loyal greetings over, the Royal Party set out for Balmoral, their route along the Quays lined by scholars from the Grammar School, Gordon's Hospital and Sheriff Watson's Industrial Schools. It was said at this time that Victoria Dock was the only dock in the entire British Empire where the royal yacht could have moored alongside a quay and where Her Majesty could have disembarked without having to be rowed ashore. The arch remained on the quayside for some years, becoming increasingly delapidated until Provost Thompson took pity on it and gave it a home at his estate of Pitmedden at Dyce.

In its early days, Waterloo Quay was described as running 'From

Harbour Entrance to the Canal to the Building Yards' (the shipyards) and had, according to William Skene, a forlorn air. In his *East Neuk Chronicles* of 1906 he writes:

From the foot of Commerce Street down to opposite the London boat shed (at the Wellington Street end) there was nothing but a wilderness of stoneyards and logs of wood. The Great North of Scotland Railway was unheard of, and it was the middle of the fifties before even the Northern Agricultural Company came into existence.

The family of John Gibb must take responsibility for the wilderness of stoneyards, indeed the versatile Gibb was the first owner of Rubislaw Quarry to appreciate the quality of its granite. The Quay,though, housed ship chandlers and spirit merchants from the start. For about ten years from 1848 one of the city's earliest co-operatives, the Footdee Baking Association which was also a grocery and run by the Footdee Savings Association, had premises there. A venture by Halls' enterprising shipwrights, it unfortunately collapsed, the result of managerial fraud. It was from Waterloo Quay that emigrants sailed direct to Canada in the *Berbice* under Captain Elliot, another Duthie brother-in-law, and the *St Lawrence* under Captain Tulloch. Those who wished could drown their sorrows at parting in one or all of the five Waterloo pubs or in any of the further nine between Wellington Street and Pocra Quay. Nevertheless, many respectable folk such as Captain Cargill,

Waterloo Quay in 1939.

John Gibb, and Alexander Duthie the shipbuilder lived on Waterloo Quay. In nearby Canal Terrace, 'a very pleasant place' before the railway sliced into it, Walter Hood the shipbuilder resided for a time as did Dr A C Matthew, physician and lemonade manufacturer, another Duthie son-in-law, while in nearby Middle Third, yet another Duthie-in-law was to be found, Captain Duncan Walker, master of the *Heroine*.

In 1854 the Northern Agricultural Company feued ground on the Quay between Church Street and Lime Street to accommodate their business 'in coals, lime, guano and other manures'. Here from their custom-built offices and warehouses they conducted their 'Cake and Manure Manufactory' - (cattle cake and bone-meal) - produced as former Church Street residents recall, to the accompaniment of considerable noise and smell. In the early 1930s the Northern Agricultural amalgamated with the Aberdeen Lime Company as Nalco. Alex Lyon and Ogston & Tennent also manufactured edible fats on the Lime Street corner.

These properties were acquired in 1972 for the Seaforth Maritime Group, then newly set up to provide offshore support vessels and other services for the new North Sea oil industry. The moving spirits of the early years were the merchant banker Ian Noble, chairman during the first five years, and James Hann a chief executive of drive and foresight. Seaforth established a supply base at their front door and the maroon livery of their offshore fleet, *Seaforth Hero, Seaforth Emperor* and half-a-dozen others became a familiar sight in the Victoria Dock.

In 1989, however, following the oil price crash, Seaforth, by then owned by James Finlay and Taylow Woodrow, disposed of its fleet to a Norwegian firm, and a management buy-out took place, led by Mr Tony Peers, who became managing director. The firm now continued its other oil-related activities including transport and diving, and in 1992, following financial recovery, resumed its original role, the management of offshore support vessels. By then Seaforth had a payroll of around 300 with a turnover of more than £15 million and the following year was acquired for £8 million by the international energy industry contractors Brown and Root, a division of the US oil services conglomerate Halliburton.

In its early days the company undertook a skilled refurbishment of the former Nalco offices and warehouses and other buildings in the area and the Seaforth complex is now a waterfront gem. It is fortunate that Tony Peers who had been the firm's logistics director and at one time its property director had a background in building technology and an appreciation of the character of the industrial archaeology of which his company had become custodians. When he took over, part of the future Seaforth Centre was still operating as a granary, acquired from the then owners Rank Hovis McDougall. 'It was,' Peers recalled, 'a very complex place, with grains trucks coming in and out,

The handsomely restored warehouse behind
Seaforth Maritime's Waterloo Quay premises.

sacks running down the chutes and so forth.' At the Lime Street corner, offal was still being rendered into one pound packs of lard. The agreement with Rank Hovis allowed this process to continue for a couple of years, perhaps not the ideal start for a firm that aimed to make a mark in the world of offshore oil.

During the major refurbishment that followed warehouses were skillfully converted in offices for Seaforth and their staff and tenants, which these days include the offices of Aberdeen Enterprise. The modern Skyline Building of 1974-75 links together two very different buildings within the complex and received a Civic Society Award, while in 1982 there followed a Commendation for the cleaning and restoration of the older buildings between Church Street and Wellington Street which by then had virtually all been acquired.

Among them were the handsome Category-B listed premises on the Wellington Street corner, No 87 Waterloo Quay. These were custom-built in 1837 for the recently established Aberdeen Steam Navigation Company which ran the famous London boats and who three years earlier had thought-fully provided a splendid shed on the quay to shelter passengers and goods alike. The company whose predecessor, established in 1707, ran smacks between Aberdeen and London, was an amalgamation of the Aberdeen Shipping Company and the Aberdeen and London Steam Navigation Company. Aberdeen Steam's early paddle boats were built by John Duffus & Co.' of whom more anon, but their later iron paddle steamers *City of London,* 1844, and the *Earl of Aberdeen,* 1846, were Clyde-built, the largest then built on that river. Of the *City of London,* 1116 tons, Lachlan Mackinnon wrote in *Recollections of an Old Lawyer* (1936):

She was one of the few transports that weathered the great gale at Balaclava Harbour during the Crimean War. Her beam of 52 feet 6 inches across the paddle-boxes was so great that she had little more than room to get through the dock entrance. She could make the run between London and Aberdeen in three tides on a huge expenditure of coal. She was described in the *Illustrated London News* of 27th July 1844, as a 'stupendous vessel....and with the exception of the *Great Britain,* which has not yet been to sea, she is the largest iron steamship afloat.'

Aberdeen Steam's 'City of London'. The comfort of dumb brutes....was not overlooked

Such was the vessel Captain John Cargill commanded These steamers sailed from Waterloo Quay, with livestock for the London market, but the company was also tourist orientated, publishing a charming booklet in 1892 entitled 'St Paul's to the Highlands and Back'. Latterly managed by Coast Lines, the London boats survived until the 1960s and if one discounts the Northern Isles run, was Aberdeen's last coastal service.

Aberdeen Steam's handsome building and its occupants narrowly missed disaster some ten years after the war when the steel shear legs opposite collapsed and crashed on to Waterloo Quay, inches from No 87. Many Aberdonians will recall this familiar quayside landmark towering skywards near the Wellington Street junction. The 'legs' were eventually removed in 1975 though they had been taken out of use some years earlier. These shears could lift 100 tons and more and had been commissioned in 1910 to lift the boilers of the *Intaba* which Hall Russell were at that time fitting out for John T Rennie's London to Durban line. It was feared that the existing wooden shear legs of 75 tons capacity might be unable to cope. In 1874 these shears had in turn replaced earlier poles constructed in 1856 and handling up to 50 tons. Such is the march of technology. A little further along, near the junction with York Place were the Dock Gates and St Clement's Bridge, opened in 1953 by the Queen Mother and taken down during Victoria Dock's conversion to full tidal working in 1975 to accommodate the round-the-clock needs of the oil industry. Here too is Dock Gates House, the harbour master's former residence, now an office.

Beside the vestiges of the old Dock Gates is the lifeboat station, official address 'Dock Island' where the RNLI's *BP Forties*, successor to the *Ramsay Dyce* is moored. She was lanched in 1976, funded by the oil company to the tune of £100,000 with £7000 from Aberdeen University students' charities for electronic equipment. The tradition that Fittie men were always to be found in the lifeboat crew continued until the 1980s. Indeed half the crew was drawn from the village as late as the 1970s. In the early days before the advent of the RNLI in the mid 1920s, virtually the whole crew consisted of Fittie pilots and the story of their bravery and their sometimes difficult relationship with the harbour authorities is related in the booklet *To the Rescue! Life-Saving at Aberdeen 1802-1924* by J L Duthie. In 1925 the RNLI took over the station at the request of the Harbour Commissioners, and that story is told in *The Lifeline: A History of the Aberdeen Lifeboat Station 1925-1985* by Norman Trewren.

Waterloo Quay terminates at the junction with York Place. Beyond lay the tidal harbour and the fishers' haven of Pocra where later the shipyards grew up. Their story is told in Part Four. Beyond the yards lay Pocra Quay at the very edge of Fittie and our next port of call.

Chapter 9

Pocra Quay: Blockhouse and Whalers

Pock, poke: a net in the form of a bag or pouch for catching salmon. Raw: a row.
Scottish National Dictionary.

To the west and south the Footdee Squares are girt by Pocra Quay. It curves from York Street to the south end of New Pier Road. This is the 'industrial' sector. Then it becomes a broad quay that faces south, across to Torry. We are now virtually at the old Sandness, at the 'public' sector, where people can park and stroll to the North Pier. Where the two sectors meet a Harbour Board plaque outlines the history: '*Pocra Quay, for centuries a haven for small fishing boats....*'

Look back and you'll see the former Hall Russell fabrication hall, now truncated and part of the harbour's multi-berth facility. This was the area of the original fisher haven or Pockraw as noted by Parson Gordon. Shipbuilding had begun here by the mid-seventeenth century and a century later, the name Pockraw (modified to Pocra by the early nineteenth century) was also being applied to points south-east. In 1755 the Town Council authorised the building of Pocraw Pier, long known as the New Pier, or 'Pear' as in Taylor's Plan of 1773. It was sited near the Blockhouse, the old fortress of Aberdeen.

In the 'industrial' sector of Pocra Quay, across from the Harbour Board's plaque sits another, a plain stone tablet, just outside the perimeter fence of the Esso Petroleum Company's Marine Plant. The inscription, cryptically and perhaps not totally accurately, indicates the progesss of the blockhouse from

97

fort to fishhouse. It reads:

1477
A FORT STOOD HERE
1532
THE BLOCK HOUSE
1879
THIS BUILDING
ERECTED

'This building' it must be said has no connection with the Esso stockade and its storage tanks. It was a tenement erected by Messrs L. Findlay & Sons, fish curers to house their workers.

Little is known of the first Blockhouse. On June 11, 1497 the magistrates decreed that for the safety of Aberdeen and the resisting of the old enemy, England, 'ane blockhouse salbe bigyt of gryt strinth at the hevin moutht'. Great strength was a moot point. There are a number of references in the Council Register to the building of blockhouses after this period. Another appears to have got underway in 1514 and on June 16 of that year there was a demand from the Council that the tax set to finance its building 'be incontinent (immediately) paid'. Every bailie was to go through his quarter rounding up non-payers, the most recalcitrant of whom would forfeit their goods. Present day councillors are doubtless grateful that they are not personally called on to hound non-payers of the council tax. Another block-house seems to have made an apearance in 1521 when revenue from the Foords (the salmon fishings on the Dee at Ruthrieston) was used to pay 'for building the Blockhouse and buying of powder and payment to the gunners fees for defense of the Town against the old Enemies of England'.

Presumably these early blockhouses were timber structures. The fort built in 1532, which appears prominently in Slezer's drawing of 'New Aberdene from the Blockhouse', page 14, was a more substantial affair, a circular building with gunloops enclosing a narrow tower with saddle-back roof. It was built in chaotic circumstances. Early in 1532, with an English invasion imminent, the Council was in the grip of panic. Who on earth had gone off with the municipal cannons? The magistrates had to find out 'quhar thair artailzerie

Slezer's drawing of the Blockhouse.

98

is, quhaus handis it is in'. The masons Pate Franche and Sanderis Monypenny were contracted to build 'in all guidlie haist....ane blokhouse of lyme and stane on the Sandness', 36 ft long, 18ft broad with walls 6 ft thick. The centres of the Bridge of Dee, 'so many as are not stolen' were to be used for the arches. Presumably all were stolen for no arches materialised. This was an ingenious attempt on the part of the magistrates to save money. The Bridge of Dee's original centres - wooden frames for arches removed after the mortar had set - had been 'brokin, spylt and away to sea' during a spate of 1522. The magistrates were clearly anxious to get good use out of the second lot.

The threat of invasion had now receded, though in 1533 the decision was taken to complete the Blockhouse whether there was war or peace with England. Parson Gordon later described this fort as 'a rough piece of work - a grosse bulk of a building'. If Pate was a member of the same family of master masons as Thomas Franche Snr. who had worked on St Machar's Cathedral and built the Bridge of Dee - which perhaps explains why the fate of its centres was readily called to mind - then perhaps he was one of the less gifted members.

Built initially to defend Aberdeen from the English and subsequently the Dutch, Spanish, French and Americans, the Blockhouse had a chequered career. In 1548 the gunpowder used was 'stirk and vehement' and liable to cause more damage to the gunners than the enemy. This was another difficult period when the town was again on the defensive against the auld enemy. But who better to be appointed keeper of the Blockhouse than the provost's son, Gilbert Menzies? He would have men to look after it 'each to have £4 in the month during the town's will' to keep the place day and night. In spite of Gilbert's efforts, the Blockhouse required extensive repairs by the 1580s and fifty chalders of lime 'fynely mixt' were provided. These the magistrates were accused of embezzling and also of letting 'the furnitur of the said blockhouse' fall into decay. That it had any at all is surprising. Delinquent Fittie fishermen Wiliam Brabner, Patrik Hucheon and James Symsoun it will be recalled had been convicted in 1601 of cutting up and removing 'ane gryt trie out of the blokhous pertening to the towne', a large log doubtless intended for its repair.

The Blockhouse now began to house the occasional civic function. In September 1602, six burgesses including Andro Rait, mariner, and two lesser mortals were quarantined there for a month having come from the 'toune of Danskine' which was 'infectit with plague'. Twenty years later it was back to defensive duties. Six guns had to be hastily mounted in 1627 - hence the importance of keeping the Futty highway free from encumbrance - when a hostile Spanish fleet, having wasted the Shetlands, was spotted off the coast. Fortunately no atttack was forthcoming. Early in the eighteenth century the old fort was reconstructed and armed with twelve pound cannon and is shown in Gregory Sharpe's 'East View of Aberdeen' of 1732 with crenellated battlement while in Milne's Plan of 1789 it appears as a sizeable fortress resembling a back-to-front E. However, its days as a working fortress would have been over by then, thanks to the North Pier.

The construction of the North Pier a few hundred yards away at the Sandness went ahead in the 1770s and by the time the first phase was completed in 1781 it was evident that the Blockhouse no longer commanded the harbour entrance. Its guns were removed and mounted in a new battery built on sandhills on the beach side of the North Pier 'upon a plan furnished by Captain Fraser, engineer for Scotland', wrote Joseph Roberston in 1839. He was not impressed. 'The expense of this structure amounted to £1200; and the total inefficiency of its appointment was speedily demonstrated'. Robertson was referring to an episode in a small war between French and American privateers, allies during the American War of Independence, and their British oponents. In a cutting out expedition on May 1781, Captain Fall commanding the *Dreadnought* of Dunkirk cheekily captured the privateers *Liberty* of Leith and *Hazard* of London lying at Aberdeen whilst their crews were relaxing ashore. The new battery's gunner was at home at the time, but 'being roused from his slumbers....ran to the battery where he found a large crowd of people who had fired off three of the guns (which fell short). He desired them to retire but they refused; and the crowd and confusion was so great that it was not possible to work the guns with effect'.

The lesson of this fiasco was not lost. At the outbreak of the French Revolutionary wars, Arthur Gibbon formed the Aberdeen Battery Company in 1794, determined that the 'harbour mouth be kept in an proper state of defence, so that the approach of enemy ships would not be succeeded by the disastrous results of 1781'. Among his many harbour interests Arthur appears to have had a ship chandlers business. He was therefore well placed to sell the shoremaster an eight guinea Dolland telescope (with case) 'for use of Battery', while the following year, 1795, 'straps to the great guns' were purchased at 11/-. Nor was Arthur's army forgotten. Coals, candles and brooms, doubtless to sweep out the sand, were regularly purchased for the Battery in the early nineteenth century.

Meanwhile, the Blockhouse, shorn of its armament, continued its civic career. In the 1760s meetings of the Aberdeen Footdee Society were held there, very opportunely since one of the members, Lewis Murray, had his vintner's business there. In 1798 it served as an auction room for sales of 'stranded goods' - unclaimed cargo. By the late 1830s the Blockhouse was partially dismantled and used, according to Robertson as a smiddy. And it had a later life as a boilhouse where whale blubber was rendered into oil.

Aberdeen entered the whaling trade early and was to enjoy, though that is not the right word, five phases of varying success over a century. It was from

Pocra that the vessels sailed. In 1752 a consortium of Aberdeen merchants and country gentlemen raised £8000 in £50 shares and fitted out two small whalers for the Greenland seas. Their first season was successful, the *Saint Ann* bringing home five whales, the *City of Aberdeen* two. The second year was disastrous with the *Saint Ann* returning home 'a clean ship', empty after being damaged by ice, and the *City of Aberdeen* with only two whales. A hiatus followed but the new pier was constructed at Pocra at this time so some expansion must have been envisaged.

The industry re-established itself in its second phase in 1783 when Arthur and James Gibbon found time among their many commitments to set up the Aberdeen Whale Fishing Company (WFC), with two vessels, the *Hercules* and *Latona,* and rented land from the Council near the Blockhouse for nineteen years at 1/- a year as a boilhouse. They had reasonable fortune, *Latona,* for example returning 'a full ship' in 1809, though she perished four years later in the Davis Strait. In 1787 Francis Leys & Co. merchants, decided to go in for whaling in a big way but probaby met with less success than they had envisaged. The land Bailie Leys had rented at Pocra was leased by the Council again in 1803 to one Alexander Fraser at £15 a year for one year - this included warehouses erected by Leys & Co. - but use as a boilhouse was strictly forbidden.

The Town's attempts to be environmentally conscious were short-lived, however. Whaling began to boom again. In 1811 the Aberdeen WFC acquired the *Diamond* and adhering to the dictum 'wer ain fish guts tae wer ain sea maws' as so many whaling interests did, appointed William Gibbon Jnr master. She was lost in 1819 after a moderately successful career and there were other misfortunes during this period. By 1812 boilhouses had begun to appear in force at Pocra, running westwards roughly according to the date of their company's foundation along the line of New Pier Road. Nearest the pier and immediately parallel to the west side of the Fisher Squares were the boilhouses of the Aberdeen WFC (1783) and the Union WFC (1802); then came the Greenland WFC (1812) whose whaler *Elbe* had a run-in that year with a privateer. With assistance from other whalers in the convoy the enemy was driven off. At the west end of York Street, were the Bon Accord WFC (1813) and the Dee WFC (1814). A & T Bannerman's company followed next in line in 1819. The plan of 1820 on page 102, shows the location of each company boilhouse. By 1820 six Aberdeen companies owned fifteen whalers all told, each with a complement of fifty men. The roster as given by Kennedy was: '1 master, 1 mate, 1 surgeon, 6 harpooners, 6 boat-steerers, 6 line-managers, 6 green men or landsmen, 6 apprentices, and 17 seamen'. The latter had other dangers to contend with apart from Arctic waters and frenzied whales. Being young, hardy and professional sailors they were considered ideal 'recruits' for His Majesty's Navy. In spite of official protection five seamen were 'pressed

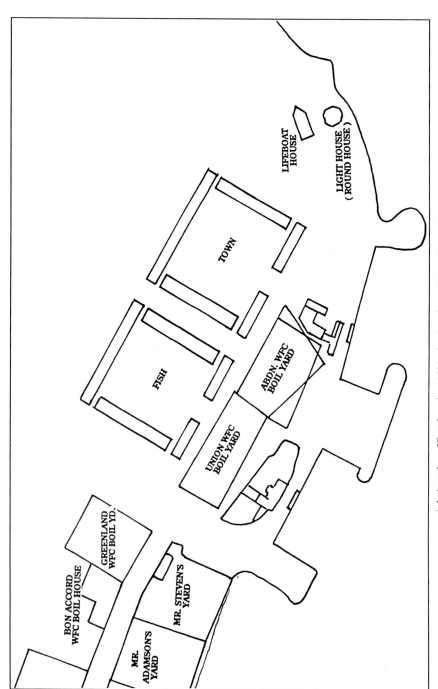

A feuing plan of Footdee, circa 1820, showing the position of the boilhouses.

LIFEBOAT
HOUSE

LIGHT HOUSE
(ROUND HOUSE)

TOWN

FISH

ABDN. WFC
BOIL YARD

UNION WFC
BOIL YARD

BON ACCORD
WFC BOIL HOUSE

GREENLAND
WFC BOIL YD.

MR. STEVEN'S
YARD

MR.
ADAMSON'S
YARD

from the *City of Aberdeen* in 1760.

The sight of some 750 men embarking in the spring at Pocra from Geenland and later the Davis Straits must have been memorable, and even more dramatic the autumn return with hundreds of barrels of blubber on the quay, not to mention the ensuing stench from the boilhouses. In 1814, 178 whales were caught by thirteen vessels, 120 by fifteen vessels in 1820, and 179 by fourteen whalers in 1823. In that last year the yield of oil was 1841 tons, the highest on record for Aberdeen. At an average of over ten tons per whale, reasonably mature beasts must have been killed. In 1826 at the peak of this third phase a new jetty was provided at Pocra to give more mooring space.

By the 1830s, however, the Greenland waters were regarded as fished out and the Union, Dee and Greenland companies put their boilhouses on the market. More vessels now went further afield to the Davis Straits and to more dangerous waters. In 1837, George Thomson, merchant, (not to be confused with George Thompson, of the Aberdeen White Star Line) brought to the attention of the Council 'the lamentable situation of crews of certain whale fishing vessels in the Davis Straits'. There were 300 souls ice-bound including the complement of the *Dee*. He suggested that the magistrates petition the Treasury to offer bounties to vessels to go there and render assistance. He also called for a 'hospital to be established at Stromness with a medical attendant and clothes and provisions for crews of such of the icebound vessels as may be so fortunate as to arrive at that port'. Bounties were indeed offered and the *Dee* eventually made landfall at Stromness in April 1837. Of her crew of forty-six there were only nine survivors.

By 1839, twelve Aberdeen whalers had been lost, mostly beset in ice, and seven were withdrawn. Only one vessel left Pocra for the Davis Straits that year, the *Bon Accord* under the renowned whaling master Captain Penny, accompanied by his Eskimo friend Eenooloo-apik who was returning to his Inuit homeland. The Eskimo had stayed with the Penny family at their home, South Polmuir Cottage on what is now Riverside Drive and had delighted crowds with his display of fishing from his canoe on the River Dee with full Eskimo gear and weaponry.

Nevertheless a fourth phase began in Aberdeen in the 1840s, but

Captain Penny, courtesy of the National Portrait Gallery.

103

only three vessels were regularly involved, the *St Andrew, Pacific* and
Flamingo, the latter two built by
William Duthie. The *St Andrew* and
Pacific owned latterly by the Aberdeen Whaling Company were both
lost in the early 1860s after several
unsuccessful trips. *Flamingo,* owned
by Provost Nicol's consortium went
to the Arctic only between 1847 and
1849 and was used exclusively for
sealing. The canny Provost had her
fitted out as a cargo ship in winter.

'Pocra Jetty about the month of
October and through the winter had,
more especially if there had been a
good fishing, a pretty strong per-
fume not exactly of Araby the Blest'.

Eenooloo-apik.

So wrote William Skene looking back to the late 1840s and 1850s. He recalled
that Fittie personality, 'Eeley' (Oiley) Betty who lived in Middle Third and
worked at a boilhouse:

> Betty invariably wore a blue blaize petticoat and whenever her crusie required
> replenishing, she divested herself of her petticoat, dipped it in the blubber vat and then
> carried it home over her arm. When she got home she wrung the oil out, hung it up for
> the night and put it on again in the morning.

Such were the perks of the job. In 1843, however, the *New Statistical
Account* noted the decline of whaling through:

> the withdrawing of the Government bounty, the reduction of duty on foreign
> seeds from which oil is made, the diminished demand for (whale) oil of late in
> consequence of the introduction of gas as a means of obtaining light and the want of
> success in the industry.

Meanwhile Captain Penny enjoyed an interlude from whaling if not from
the Davis Strait when he sailed in 1850 in search of Sir John Franklin. Nothing
had been heard of Franklin's expedition since he set out in 1843 to find the
North West passage, and the quest to discover what had happened to it was
now gripping the nation. Penny's ships, the *Lady Franklin*, built in Walter
Hood's yard, and the *Sophia*, had been financed by Lady Franklin and though
his search was unsuccessful, Penny's friendship with the Franklin family

continued. It was possibly a result of this contact that in 1854 both ships were bought by a new whaling and sealing firm, the Aberdeen Arctic Company of which Penny was general superintendent. The *Alibi* was added in 1856 and she slaughtered a total of 7000 seals that season. This company, although managed by that hard-headed Footdee merchant William Hogarth, had altruistic aims towards the Eskimaux whom Penny was convinced were being debauched by European and American influences. The company had reasonable success in whaling and sealing if not in proselytising, but was wound up in 1865. *Sophia*, Aberdeen's last surviving whaler then went trading to Archangel. So ended Aberdeen's fifth and final phase as a whaling port although an interesting visitor discharging at Pocra during the 1860s was the *Daniel Webster* whaler of New Bedford whose master thought the better of returning home during the American Civil War.

Whaling had always been a very speculative trade as well as a dangerous and brutal one. The wreck of the *Oscar* in 1813, caught on a lee shore and driven onto rocks round in Greyhope Bay with the loss of all but two of a forty-four man crew perhaps brought home the dangers more vividly than reports of ships lost in far off Arctic waters.

The famous North Boats were also based at Pocra for a few years until the mid 1880s. The firm started off in the late eighteenth century as the Leith and Clyde Shipping Company and after amalgamation became the Aberdeen, Leith, Clyde and Tay Shipping Company in 1810. With routes to the far north established, the firm in 1875 changed its name to yet another tongue twister, the North of Scotland Orkney and Shetland Steam Navigation Company many of whose famous ferries would be built by Hall Russell. This expanding venture required more space and in 1884 left Pocra for the newly developed Provost Matthew's Quay across on the Inches. Taken over by P & O Shipping in 1971, the North Boats sail these days as P&O Ferries from the Upper Dock.

Whaling is associated with Pocra Quay, cows are not. In 1881, however, the east coast of Scotland was opened to the importation of Canadian livestock and Pocra Jetty down at the York Street end of the quay became a government approved landing place. On arrival, to avoid disruption at the quay, the cattle were driven over a bridge to sheds where the MGIT offices are now based. A small mart was built where farmers foregathered on auction day, and in 1890, the Board of Agriculture approved a slaughter house and fodder shed. From time to time cattle broke loose, and the story is told of one beast which escaped and ran into a house in the Squares where a quick-thinking lad shouted: 'Shut the door mither, it'll dae us a winter.' The venture ended in 1893 when a prohibition order was issued folllowing a disease scare.

Further along the quay, the Torry Ferry embarked from the Lower Jetty. It was handily placed for the Steam Yacht Inn and particularly for the Ferry

TS Scylla, the Sea Cadets headquarters.

Boat Tavern whose landlords - Willie Cormack was the best known - also ran the ferry. Aberdeen Sea Cadets now have their HQ on this site in a complex of Nissen huts, inherited from the last war. During the 1870s, the magistrates received memorials from Fittie residents both for and against the withdrawal of licences from these public houses. The battle swung to and fro, with the shipbuilders on the side of temperance.

With the improvements advised by Telford at last implemented, the treacherous channel tamed, the mud flats or Inches now dry land, the Albert Basin created and reclaimed land made available for industry following the Dee's diversion, Aberdeen by the 1870s was able to offer the booming east coast herring fishery wharfage and space for curing yards. The former Inch of Point Law was the mecca of the seasonal yards, but a number of interests were based at Pocra on a permanent basis. Among these were John R Nutman, fish merchants from Great Yarmouth, and the fishcurers, Overall & Co., as well as locals William Walker and William Davidson.

The Blockhouse, its days as a boilhouse over and now in ruins, found itself a victim of joint indignities. It was encompassed by a timber yard and consequently had an address, Nos 14-18 Pocra Quay. In 1877 this yard was taken over by Lewis Findlay & Sons, fishcurers from Johnshaven. At that time, the blockhouse ruins were finally removed and replaced by Findlay's Build-

106

The site of the Blockhouse at Pocra Quay

ings, a tall tenement built to house Findlay's workers. It was then that the city's Dean of Guild, Alexander Walker erected the tablet on his own initiative to mark the site of the old fort.

Findlay employed workers all year round, curing herring for the Continent during the summer, and buying haddock from the Fittie line fishers in the winter for his dried fish trade to Africa and South America. His complex also included the Farlins, sheds where the Fittie women guttted fish and there was a cooperage at the York Street end. Pocra in the late nineteenth century was indeed a busy place, offering work and accommodation. Important harbour folk also lived on the quay though nearer the Round House. During the 1870s and 1880s, these included the Pilot Master (Harbour Master) William Clark, and the Harbour Engineer William Dyce Cay who may have been a nephew of the great artist, William Dyce. The latter had a brother-in-law Cay and the dates correspond.

Pocra Quay was widened in 1904 and six years later bunkering facilities were provided for the Grand Fleet, signs of growing unease with the Kaiser's Germany. Later, in peace time, bunkering services were to become available for oil burning and diesel vessels. The Johnstone Oil Depot was based here from the 1930s and eventually took over Findlay's Building as offices. This gaunt though handsome tenement, where Ruby Webster's mother would send her with a 'fry' for some of the later tenants, was allowed to run down and

107

Pocra Quay 1974.

Pocra Quay 1993. The Army of Martians.

vanished in the 1970s. Esso is now based on this site.

By the early 1970s, at the beginning of the oil boom, Pocra Quay offered a new and fantastic sight, a forest of huge silos gleaming red and yellow, belonging to the mud firms, Milchem, Baroid, Dressser-Magcobar and IMC . As a deep water berth with no tidal restrictions, Pocra Quay was to prove as popular with the oil companies as it had done with the warring factions in Spalding's day in the seventeenth century, and the whalers of the nineteenth. But the old patched-up timber quay was now deteriorating rapidly. It was 'stood down' in 1982 by the Harbour Board and replaced by New Pocra Quay the following year offering the complete range of facilities sought by both offshore supply boats, and general cargo ships. In 1982 there were objections to the silos on environmental grounds, and as recounted in Chapter 4, there were further objections in 1992 when this army of Martian structures, now a uniform navy blue, seemed poised to invade New Pier Road. Planning permission for this encroachment was refused. Hopefully incoming industry will respect the peace and well-being of residents and the two will live amicably side by side as other industries and other Fittie folk have done in the past.

Aberdeen by William Daniell, 1822. Note the Round House on Pocra Quay and the Fish Town behind.

Chapter 10

Pocra Quay: Round House and North Pier

Immense operations have begun to render Aberdeen a great commercial port. Superb piers have been constructed at its entrance.
C Dupin (a distinguished French marine engineer) 1817

And now we turn into the spacious south side of Pocra Quay, prominent in William Daniell's engraving of Aberdeen in 1822. At the junction of the quay and the North Pier stands the Round House, its red roof in Daniell's print surmounted by a turret that commmands harbour and bay. The octagonal 'Round' House, though unnamed, is scrupulously drawn in Colin Innes's Plan of Footdee of 1803 which makes it Fittie's oldest building. But how old? There is some difficulty in pinning down the year of erection for although familiarly known as the Round House, and nowadays officially as the Navigation Control Centre, it appears as 'Observatory' on maps well into the twentieth century and seems not to have had an official name at time of completion. However the Shoremaster's Accounts for 1797-98 show an expenditure of £225 5s on the 'New House lately Built at the North Pier'. This could well be it. In 1793, the Footdee Society received a tender for seven houses, 17ft by 15ft, all for £100. These would have be humble dwellings but for £225 5s one would expect a substantial structure. The 1797-98 Accounts also show the purchase of 'Telescope of the Lookout House of the North Pier' at ten guineas. Moreover I can't help wondering if there was an architectural affinity with the octagonal Hermitage of Powis which was built of similar material in 1781 at a cost of £149 8s 1d and also designed to spy out the land, and John Ewen's Hermitage of the same era at Polmuir.

Many Aberdonians will recall how the Round House used to control harbour traffic in times gone by, the outward and visible sign of which was a

111

signalling mast up and down which three black balls ran to indicate whether the harbour was open or closed. Those bold enough to venture in against the signal would be angrily reprimanded by a disembodied voice booming from the hailing station, 'Fit's adee wi ye skipper, can ye nae see,' while a call of, 'Where ye bound for?' would invite departing vessels to disclose their next port of call. All this is past history, and to their great credit, when modernisation was carried out in 1966, the Harbour Board, instead of adding a modern excresence, extended the Round House upwards, and it is the top floor which houses a panoply of 'high tech' equipment controlling harbour navigation lights and signals. The famous black balls have been superseded by a high intensity electric system while the harbour's VHF radio system communicates with harbour traffic. A 'Paper Book ruled for use of Birthmaster' purchased in 1794 by the shoremaster from Alex. Brown, Bookseller, would two centuries on, prove rather inadequate. Some 11,000 ships now arrive annually and the port is one of Aberdeen's most successful enterprises. It was at the Round House in August 1986 that the Queen unveiled one of Pocra's famous plaques. This one commemorates Aberdeen harbour's 850 years as a going concern.

The harbour pilots, all master mariners are based in the middle floor of the Round House while the pilot cutter ties up at Pocra Quay. It's a long time since the Fittie and Torry fishermen had the monolopy on pilotage. From 1810 pilots had to be licensed, and by 1922 strict bye-laws were implemented as to qualifications and competency. The pilots remained self-employed until the mid 1980s. Although no pilots live in Pilot Square these days, the stalwarts of

The North Pier. The Silver Darling Restaurant, left, with 'Scarty's Monument' in the distance..

another harbour elite, Billy Cowper and George Walker long-serving harbour boatmen live in the Squares, and remain self-employed. The boatmen, also licensed by the Board, attend to the mooring of ships. Their headquarters are in the one-storey crenellated former customs watch house a building which they share somewhat unexpectedly with the Silver Darling, a Seafood Restaurant that cooks in the French style, its name inspired by the statuette of Grace Darling on the roof, and the term for a herring.

Adjoining the boatmen's headquarters is a store that until 1986 was the salmon fishers' station. Before improvements to the navigation channel in the later nineteenth century could begin, the salmon fishings in the Dee estuary, the Raik and Stell fishings, operated jointly by the nineteenth century, and the Midchingle fishings had to be bought out by the Harbour Commissioners. This took place in 1871 at a cost of £30,000. (Seventy years earlier a questionnaire 'presented by Mr Telford for the Magistrates of Aberdeen' with answers signed by Provost James Hadden valued the fishings at £80,000 -£100,000!) After harbour improvements were completed and the Dee diverted the salmon fishings were seen as a valuable harbour asset and netting was resumed, though not in the Raiks and Stells which had been replaced by the Albert Basin where no self-respecting salmon would be found, nor in the Midchingle which had disappeared under South College Street. The stances were regrouped with three nets inside the South Breakwater, three south of the South Breakwater, and eighteen more north of the North Pier. By the time the Atlantic Salmon Conservation Trust bought out the nets in the 1980s with the aim of improving the salmon run upstream, salmon fishers George Ritchie and Levi Forbes had sixty years service between them, working with net and coble and bag annually between February 11 and September 30. The picturesque sight of these fishermen tending to their nets and cobles outside the Round House has probably vanished forever.

Returning to the area of Daniell's print, some twentieth century additions to Pocra Quay deserve comment. Facing the harbour in marked contrast with the masonry of nearby New Pier Road and Pilot Square is a short row of early twentieth century granite villas, probably by the Woodside builder Joseph Shirras. The largest, North Pier House was once the residence of the Assistant Harbour Master. Fittie's War Memorial is prominently sited on the quay, a fine piece of work by a local man, John Caie of the Pittodrie

The War Memorial.

113

'Scarty's Monument'.

Granite Works, which fittingly commemorates mariner as well as soldier.

'Scarty's Monument', a rather down-market brick obelisk stands at a discreet distance. 'Scarty' was the tee name of William Smith one of two pilots, the other being James Morrice or 'Pengie' who kept watch from the North Pier during rough weather in the middle years of the nineteenth century. Both men were great jokers. 'Pengie' coming off watch to receive communion at St Clement's Church one Sunday noted that the officiating elder was the director of a local shipping company whose Sunday working was frowned on by the minister. 'Pengie,' whispered the elder anxiously as he placed the holy cup in front of him, 'is the Newcastle boat in yet?' Pengie, alas does not have a monument, but Scarty's is in fact the ventilator shaft for a sewer which still empties into the navigation channel though plans have long been in the air to direct the sewage to the long sea outfall at Nigg. A poem by Anon has been written in honour of the monument:

> I'll tell you o a Monument
> Erected in this Toon.
> It stands doon by the Fisher Squares
> An built wi bricks a roon.
> Oh it would look much better
> If they'd geint a coat o paint
> And stuck a brass plate on the front
> O Skarty's Monument.

And so it continues for several further verses of increasingly lavatorial humour.

Adjoining the Round House is the North Pier where Scarty spent so much time and whose foundation stone 'was laid at the Sandness with masonic solemnities 'in June 1775. It was the brain child of the famous Yorkshire engineer John Smeaton who was commissioned in 1769 to advise how the harbour entrance could be enlarged to encourage shipping. Problems included lack of water at the bar; a shifting bed of sand and gravel on the north side of the entry; and the dumping of their deposits in the estuary by the meandering Dee and Denburn. 'The erection of the North Pier,' wrote Smeaton, 'will cure the evil complained of; for it will not only keep the land freshets (streams) more confined till they come into deeper water, but will in a great measure prevent the sand and gravel from being driven in'. This, the first section of the North Pier was 1200ft long and cost £180 but an unwelcome side effect of its success was that heavy easterly swells could now race up the navigation channel and damage shipping. Hearing that Smeaton was in Montrose, Bailie Black and a Mr Carnegie sped from Aberdeen in a chaise hired at a cost of £4 11s 6d to seek his advice. Smeaton recommended a catch-

Contemporary view of Pocra Quay showing the same area as in Daniell's print of 1822. Note how the Round House and the Fish Town have grown upwards.

pier and the magistrates were impressed. The shoremaster's accounts for 1787-88 show:

£57 - Paid Mr Smeaton, Engineer for his expence in coming here and for his Trouble in inspecting the Harbour and Piers and giving his advice in relation to some proposed improvements to the Harbour and for a gratuity to him for the success that has attended the execution of the North Pier.

And so Abercrombie's Jetty was constructed in 1789 immediately below the Round House, to inhibit the swells. Unfortunately it was not the success envisaged, indeed proved a hazard to shipping and was itself removed. A stump remains and if you balance precariously enough you can read Pocra's fourth inscription: *Jno (John) Abercrombie Provost 1789* in whose honour it was named.

The first phase of the North Pier was complete in 1781, but work continued nearby. The Shoremaster's Accounts reveal additional construction work at Pocra in 1791-92. Two years later Alexander Gildavie, mason, was paid three guineas 'in going to Leith to inspect the manner of constructing Docks', and for his 'Plan of the New Pier and Bason at Pocra and moving the stone for building the same'. (Gildavie did rather better in 1798, being paid £50 for building the bridge over the Cults Burn). The accounts also show that the inner man was not neglected. There are several payments 'for Breakfast at Langlades to the Harbour Committee', one following an inspection of the North Pier, one along with 'Beer and Biscuit to the Workmen'.

An even greater depth of water at the bar and in the navigation channel was a continuing priority, and the North Pier was extended 900 ft between 1810 and 1816, a dangerous undertaking in deep, turbulent water. 'It is absolutely necessary that a resident engineer be engaged who is experienced in conducting similar works,' Telford told the Harbour Trustees. He recommended John Gibb, and the Falkirk-born engineer was engaged at £200 per annum, until what he described as 'an arduous work' was completed. Gibb whom we have already met at Waterloo Quay was quick-tempered with a trenchant vocabularly, but liked and respected by his men. Writers of the time spoke highly of his skill and integrity. Gibb worked closely with the 'Town's Superintendent' John Smith who designed the Squares, and his son was to marry Smith's daughter.

Unfortunately the end of this second section, at the North Pier sloped out into the water and rocks at its base proved the undoing of several storm-tossed vessels attempting entry. The *Ossian* in 1822, the *Grampian* in 1830, the *Brilliant* in 1839 and the *Velocity* in 1848 were all wrecked there, but most heart-rending of all was the wreck of the London Boat, the iron paddle steamer the *Duke of Sutherland* which broke in two on April 1, 1853 while attempting to cross the bar. The lifeboat was quicky on the scene, manned by Fittie pilots, Allan, Caie,

117

A print of 1853, showing the wreck of the Duke of Sutherland at the North Pier.

Main, Morrice and others, and they saved sixteen lives in spite of the lifeboat being badly damaged. Eleven were drowned from the steamer including the Captain, Edward Howling, a Mr Burness returning from the Australian gold diggings who 'had all but reached his destination', and Miss Bremner whose fiancé, a local lawyer awaited her on the pier. She 'had her bride's cake and marriage trousseau with her', reported William Skene. Equally poignant was the death of the second mate, Peter Ligertwood whose aunt was married to Captain Howling. He had already been saved but attempted to return to the shipwreck with five other volunteers who set out in a salmon coble after the lifeboat was put out of action. It was overwhelmed in heavy seas and five of the men lost. Skene gives an account of activities on the beach nearby which before night came:

> was strewn with the most heterogeneous mass of goods including parasols galore for the summer season....a large quantity of cheeses, oranges etc. and upon the principle of 'What's found's free', everybody started to help themselves....The military were called out to form a cordon along the beach and fires were lighted but in spite of every precaution great quantities of articles were taken away. Numbers of them were hidden in sandbanks along the shore and when the thieves proceeded to disinter the goods, they could not indentify the hiding places and bundles of decayed ribbons and umbrellas and parasol frames were found among the sand years afterwards.

The third and final section, 500ft long, completed the North Pier in 1879. At its end, Pocra's fifth plaque commemorates:

Sir Alexander Anderson Knt
Lord Provost.
Patrick Cooper Esqr
Master of Shore-works.
MDCCCLXV.

This lattter date, 1865, is curious since the foundation stone was not laid until September 1874.

When open to the public the North Pier's 2600ft affords a bracing and spectacular promenade. Changes in the stonework, clearly visible from the Torry side are a testament to the toil, the skill and the controversies of the past two hundred years.

The lighthouse at the end of the North Pier.

Chapter 11

The Hinterland

Taking the railway on the west and the south, and the Bannermill on the north as the limits of the district, there are about 2000 mechanics employed in Footdee, and their number will now increase.

Aberdeen Journal, November 8, 1865

In Chapter One we looked at the route from the Castlegate to Pocra as it would have been in the seventeenth and eighteenth centuries. In this chapter it might be interesting to go over much the same ground, looking at later developments many of which are still within living memory. Hangman's Brae, it will be recalled, linked up with the Summer Road, which by mid-nineteenth century had become Summer Lane. On its north-east side the Aberdeen New Gas Light Company had set up on the great expanse of the 'Sandy Ground of Futt Dee' or the 'Sandy Lands' in the 1840s and Cotton Street was laid out running from Summer Lane to the Links soon after. Aberdeen Corporation acquired the gas undertaking in 1871 and began expanding its premises there.

In these days gas was produced from coal and during the carbonisation process, unwanted tarry and liquid constituents were given off. John Miller, a Glasgow chemical entrepreneur, had arrived in Aberdeen in 1848 four years after the Gas Company had come into being and began to manufacture by-products from this unpleasant though valuable waste. He set up his Sandilands Chemical Works next door to the gasworks where he made amonia-based products such as fertiliers and coal tar from this waste, paying the Corporation in the 1880s for example 1/- per ton for 'amoniacal liquor.' By 1891 he had persuaded the Corporation to rename Summer Lane in his honour.

His son, J P Miller studied chemistry in Berlin and was for many years a director at Sandilands which he ran in the same innovative and paternalistic way as his father. The firm built tenements in and around Miller Street and Baltic Street to house their workers, the rent being collected by the Sandilands

Engineers at Sandilands Chemical Works. Courtesy, Aberdeen Art Gallery and Museums Collection.

clerks. J P Miller died in 1938, ten years after the firm had been acquired by ICI to join its newly established subsidiary, the fertiliser company SAI. The march of progress has, however, been unkind to Sandilands. Natural gas has ended the by-product industry and 'greening' philosophy and EC agricultural policy has caused the bottom to fall out of the chemical fertilisers business. SAI finally stopped trading in 1991. Innovative as ever, Sandilands soldiers on as Scotoil Services Ltd., and now wholly owned by ICI has converted its mill to produce barite for the offshore mud industry and undertakes the handling and warehousing of chemicals.

The former railway bridge nearby at the Castle Terrace/Fish Street junction, built originally by Abernethy of Ferryhill in 1863, and replaced by the current bridge in 1928 is still known as the Tarry Briggie, and the main Miller Street-St Clement Street thoroughfare has long been called the 'Tarry' because both were tarmacadamed long before this process became commonplace, and a novelty given that much of Footdee was, and remains cassied. (The handsome deep pink cassies of Clarence Street must be the finest in Aberdeen). My own suspicion is that J P Miller could have been using his street to display his product. Perhaps it paid dividends for the firm subsequently tar macadammed Anderson Drive.

In 1886 the Corporation obtained Parliamentary powers to construct a railway to replace the horse and carts that had until then conveyed coal to the gasworks. It was to run from Waterloo Quay to Miller Street via Church Street. Fittie folk were up in arms. The rail would be carried past St Clement Street School's side entrance, and scholars might be knocked down. The School Board made a 'remonstrance'. There were problems too about the Church Street incline, and squabbles amongst the Corporation, the Harbour Commissioners and the GNSR over the cost of strengthening the harbour track. Permission was obtained, however, and residents had to put up with a locomotive chuffing and belching as it pulled coal wagons along their main street. In order to avoid accidents and congestion, the 'Gasworks Railway' initially operated at night, a mixed blessing. Ethel Kilgour who lived in Church Street in the 1930s recalls the locomotive and its wagons making the houses rattle at night, but moving slowly during the day, when working must have been permitted at a later date. John Gillanders who was on the clerical staff at the gasworks recalls ordering the requisite number of coal wagons always on the evening before they were required, and always in multiples of eight from the Craiginches sidings. To this day the rails remain, suddenly vanishing into a wall in Miller Street. Looking back to his Cotton Street childhood, Albert Elrick recalls all the windows covered with multi-coloured vapour from the gasworks. It was a fact of life that was accepted.

The joint smell from the gasworks and Sandilands would have registered

Church Street looking towards Waterloo Quay. The Lime Quay was at the far end.
The rails remain.

This detail from a lithograph of 1889 by Andrew Gibb & Co. makes an interesting comparison with the Birds Eye View on page 86. On the left the railway has replaced the Canal while top left, the new St Clement's Free Kirk has opened for worship. To its right are Fish and Cotton Streets, and on the extreme right, the Gasworks are in business, with Sandilands Chemical Works below. The long buildings on the Links are the Ropeworks, and to their left, behind St Clement's Church, the lums of Blaikie Bros. Footdee Iron Works belch forth smoke. Below the Church, Links Street runs eastwards. Bottom centre, on Waterloo Quay the shear legs are prominent, with a London boat moored nearby. Courtesy, Arthur McCombie.

higher on the Richter Scale of Smells, if such a thing existed, than Aberdeen's notorious Torry pong. That was, and once in a blue moon still is fishy. The Upper Fittie pong was more sinister in that it was gaseous, nauseating, bad enough to render the Fittie end of the Beach a 'no go' area. Nor did the pipes and drums of these industries enhance the westerly aspect of our beloved seafront. There were considerable environmental improvements in 1974, however, when the gasworks were dismantled. British Gas still retains a presence in the area though their modern district office, fronting on to Links Road, takes up a fraction of the old site.

The well known furniture removal firm, the Shore Porters, established officially in 1498, though in existence prior to that date probably originated in Fittie where work was to be had for the locals, carrying goods from the quays into town. The job seems to have been open to men and women alike, the only qualification being the prowess to carry a hundredweight on the back from the Blockhouse to Broad Street, a task unlikely to daunt the average fishwife. In 1877 the firm acquired stables in Cotton Street and one of their members, James Chrystall erected six new tenements on the north side, opposite the stables to provide accommodation for his men. Albert Elrick still recalls the boyhood thrill of 'stealing' a surreptitious hurl on the Shore Porters carts and finding himself once miles away in Torry. Cotton Street's tenements were demolished in 1975 but the Shore Porters' premises remain. The city's archaeological unit is now based in Cotton Street, as is an artists' studio.

We now move down Miller Street to St Clement Street to examine the territory between Garvock Wynd and Links Street. This, of course, was the old glebe of St Clement's Church, shown clearly on Taylor's and Milne's Plans of 1773 and 1789 respectively and which even in early nineteenth century was still largely agricultural with a part let out for grazing. Nevertheless, the glebe's erosion by industry began early. Milne's Plan shows a ropery within its bounds which would run parallel with the future Links Street, while Colin Innes's Plan of 1803 shows the Society of Cloth Manufacturers in the middle of the glebe on the north, or Garvock Wynd side, and indeed a weaver was at this time a member of the Footdee Society. Across the road a garden owned by Provosts Leys and Brebner had been earmarked for the future Church Street which was laid out in 1816. It provided a short cut from the Lime Quay, taking industry into the heart of Footdee .

Towards the end of the 1820s the works of John Duffus & Co were *in situ* on the old glebe. Duffus's description of himself as 'Engine Maker' or 'Mechanist' stands out boldly against the ubiquitous 'Merchant' of his fellow magistrates and it is interesting to note that his acquisition of the glebe was more or less contemporary with St Clement's becoming *quoad sacra* , a parish in its own right. Duffus & Co. were succeeded on the glebe site in 1845 by Blaikie Brothers' Iron Works which is shown in the lithograph opposite, lums smoking away, almost engulfing the church. The important contributions of John Duffus and the Blaikies to our industrial history are discussed in the next chapter, and we resume the story in 1900 when John Fleming & Co. Ltd., timber merchants took over this four and a half acre site vacated now by Blaikie Brothers.

John Fleming had established his sawmills at Albert Quay in 1884 on land owned by the Harbour Commissioners. Demand for timber was booming and Flemings by the 1890s were the biggest wood merchants in Aberdeen. From 1894 onwards however, Fleming had a series of arguments with the Commissioners (in spite of being one himself) over the Albert Quay rent. In March 1900 matters came to a head when Fleming described the most recent increase as 'exorbitant' while the Commissioners, in no way impressed by the fact that Fleming was Lord Provost, argued that he was using his position to get a 'cheap bargain'. John Fleming now washed his hands of the Commissioners and negotiated the purchase of the former Blaikie site for his sawmill that year. The firm made the move in 1903 and long remained a familiar part of the

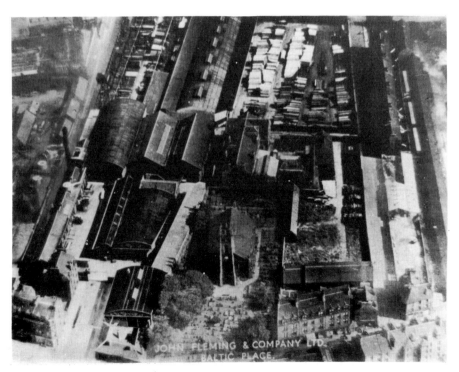

John Fleming's Baltic Place premises in the 1950s. Note St Clement's Church,centre. Courtesy of John Fleming & Co.Ltd.

landscape, subsequently expanding by purchasing land at nearby St Clement's Court and moving into Links Street when tenements there were demolished.

In 1903, the Town Council agreed to the naming of the Fleming complex as Baltic Place. Baltic Street was nearby and Sir John as he became in 1908, was no doubt mindful of the major source of his imports. After his death in 1925 expansion continued under his son Frank Fleming who guided the firm through the inter-war years, with an able lieutenant in the larger than life company secretary James Porter. Roger Fleming, Frank's son, joined the firm in 1937 and by the mid-1950s was at the helm. Timber in the post-war era was now being imported from all manner of exotic places, Scandanavia, Malaysia, Japan and South America as well as the Baltic. Roger's son Mark, who trained as a chartered accountant, joined the firm in 1974 as the fourth generation Fleming and subsequently succedeed his late father as managing director. In recent years the whole character of the timber trade has changed and Fleming's have kept pace with these changes. The Baltic Place sawmill closed after sawmilling was centralised at Grangemouth and by 1991 the entire Baltic Place staff had moved to the spacious Bridge of Don premises which the firm had acquired in 1975. For a time the Royal Coat of Arms (the firm are Royal Warrant holders) languished forlornly as sole custodian of Baltic Place but it too has 'relocated' and the former St Clement's glebe is now occupied by Rowco International's Aberdeen Freight Centre.

The ropery on Milne's Plan ran parallel with Links Street after the latter was laid out, and was subsequently extended to the Links. It became part of the Blaikie Brothers empire but was later sold off as a separate entity. Ethel Kilgour lived on the other side of Links Street, and she can still recall the whirring of machinery from a later successor on the site, the Gourock Rope Works.

Most streets in this area between Castle Terrace and the St Clement Street-Links Street junction have vanished. Opposite the former Sandiland Chemical Works the streets on the west side of Miller Street - Canal Terrace, the latter much truncated by the railway, Yeats Lane, Prince Regent Street and Garvock Street - have been replaced by the Miller Street Industrial Estate with its prefabricated warehouses of paint wholesalers and the like, all nicely landscaped. Further along, the area between the former Garvock Street and Church Street is occupied by builders' merchants and is now Unit 9 Miller Street. Across the road, the area from Sandilands to Garvock Wynd, once a densely populated stretch containing the tenements of Baltic Street and Catto Square has gone, as has Links Street, nicknamed the 'Jungle' after the Lyons family who lived there. This street largely consisted of brick houses, 'the brickies', and at different times, had also housed the St Clement's Chemical Works and a fish preserving works. On the corners however, were two early

127

York Street in 1889 from the lithograph by Andrew Gibb & Co. The shipyards are in the foreground with Duthies left, and Halls right. Opposite are a mixture of residences and industrial premises. Note the timber yard left, Neptune Terrace centre, the sawmills right and the ropeworks on the links behind. Courtesy of Arthur McCombie.

nineteenth century granite tenements, No 2 where Ethel Kilgour spent part of her childhood above Jock Wood's licensed grocery shop, and its opposite number, No 1, containing the St Clement's Bar which survives in solitary state. Upper Fittie teemed with life. There were children everywhere and even the palatial schools of the neighbourhood had difficulty in coping. Many of the tenements had poor or non-existent sanitation and overcrowding was a major problem. In 1899 the Rev Arthur Donaldson of St Clement's United Free petitioned the Corporation to provide additional housing, but the plea was not acted on at that time. Wages were low, but those in employment considered themselves fortunate. There was great neighbourliness, disadvantaged young folk had not then been invented and one event still recalled with happy memories was the Fittie Picnic, by courtesy of Mr Pearson of Reid & Pearson, the St Nicholas Street drapers. (This should not be confused with the Fittie Squares' picnic whose residents, owner-occupiers and fisherfolk to boot, were considered by the Upper Fittie folk to be a race apart). The Upper Fittie picnic was organised by the local street bookies, the Forbeses, 'Auld Beggie' and later, his son, 'Young Beggie'. Twenty or more single deckers lined Miller Street and St Clement Street and the entire population would be transported to Ellon or the Black Dog for an eagerly anticipated day of fun and games.

We move on now to York Street, developed on the line of the old Pocra

St Clement's Bar is the only surviving building in Links Street. On the left, the Northern Co-op shops on the ground floor in the course of demolition.

129

Road around 1825. On the south side the shipyards, discussed in the ensuing chapters, fronted on to the former fishers' haven. The north side, backing on to the Links, provided an interesting mix of the commercial and the residential, as shown on page 128. At the west end, Davidson's School pre-dated York Street, and therefore stood a little behind the line of the road at the rear of the present Neptune Bar. Moving eastwards, one would have found in the 1850s, the yard of Donaldson Rose, timber merchant and shipowner, while Alexander Brownie dominie at Davidson's School virtually lived 'over the shop' at No 10. Mrs Howling who took in lodgers, and her niece Mrs Peterwood Ligertwood were at No 41. Both women were widowed when the *Duke of Sutherland* foundered in 1853. Mrs Alexander Hall formerly Elizabeth Cochar, daughter, wife, mother and grandmother of shipbuilders, lived at No 45. She died in 1860 at the age of eighty-four some eleven years after her husband. Here too lived Alexander Morgan, foreman at Halls who may have been the father of Alexander Hall Morgan, shipbuilder of Whampoa, the yard near Canton established by a former Halls' apprentice, James Couper, later of Craigiebuckler. There is a tablet commemorating A H Morgan on the wall of St Clement's Churchyard beside the Hall family memorials.

At No 47 an arch led through to Nepture Terrace which existed as a commerical and residential enclave off York Street, even before gaining a separate identity in the early 1860s. (Another interesting enclave, Waterside, almost directly opposite on the shipyard side is discussed in Chapter 13). During this era, spirit dealers, carpenters, ropemakers, blockmakers, grocers, engineers, blacksmiths and shipmasters were all resident in York Street, many having their businesses there.

The Dee Iron Works of the shipbuilders, Vernon Bowman were established at the 'Squares' end of the street in 1837, and were subsequently replaced by a boat building yard and by the Footdee Sawmills. From 1878 the latter firm was run by John Rust & Co. Three generations of 'Roosties' carried on the business until the mid 1930s, and members of the family also distinguished themselves locally in other walks of life. In the later part of the nineteenth century Rust & Co. imported timber shipped in their own sailing vessels bought from the firm of John Duthie. Of these, the *John Duthie* became *Lumberman's Laddie* in 1888 while the *Windsor Castle*, originally owned by Donaldson Rose became the *Lumberman's Lassie*. By the beginning of the twentieth century the boatbuilding yard had been replaced by the Bon Accord Sawmills, immediately adjacent to the Footdee Sawmills. Near 'Roosties' Coullie's Opening also gave access to the Links. The Websters remember five cottages there built of whitewashed brick, with red tiles which were said to be haunted. At the very end, where the delapidated wooden shelter now stands, there was a big 'tarry' house, with steps leading down. Here 'Eylie Mary' shelled mussels and sold them as bait to those fishing off Pocra Quay.

Looking west along York Street towards the former Halls' sheds. Coullies Opening lay alongside. The 'tarry house' was beside the bus shelter.

Today York Street is still a wide boulevard, but little remains of the bustle and industry of a century ago. At the west end, York Street Nursery School, as noted earlier, is surrounded by a transport firm. Next to the school there stood the house of the Hall Russell shipyard manager, now gone. Across York Place, the Neptune Bar happily survives, one of Fittie's three holsteries, the St Clements Bar and the Fittie Bar being the others. Next door to the Neptune, the former Hall Russell Works Canteen is becoming increasingly derelict. Moving further eastwards, Mobil Oil North Sea Ltd now have premises in the gap of Seggie's Opening that once gave access to the Links and to Seggie's coal yard. Further along, Neptune Terrace survived until the 1960s, and the Websters still have pleasant memories of the houses within this court, tall tenements and cottages, and a bust of Neptune that perhaps came from a whaler. Like Seggie's Opening and Coullie's Opening, the rear of Neptune Terrace gave access to the Links. The Websters recall how Hall & Co. would provide local bairns with wood for Guy Fawkes bonfires there and how the 'Neptunes', the boys of Neptune Terrace, would raid the stockpiles of the Fittie loons and vice versa. Another pleasant memory of the Websters is of the York Street trough which operated at two levels, the lower for dogs, the upper for horses.

Neptune Terrace was flanked by the premises of the shipbuilders, Hall Russell to the west, and Halls to the east, including their joiner and pattern shops and the drawing office. In the 1960s Hall Russell absorbed the land that Neptune Terrace stood on, as well as the various Hall & Co. properties. The old Halls' drawing office later housed the Hall Russell apprentices' training school. The Aberdeen Industrial Training Centre is now based there, training young people in a variety of technical skills.

As one would expect in a fishing and shipbuilding community, ropemaking was one of Fittle's oldest industries. Behind the north side of York Street lay the Fittie Links and their ropeworks. As early as 1758, long before York Street had replaced the Pocra Road, Geo Tower & Co. were permitted by the magistrates to cover their ropewalk there 'to the space of fifty fathoms in length' during the continuance of their lease. James Gibbon & Co. was established nearby before 1801. In that year the firm sold the Shoremaster 'two new ropes for working vessels into harbour in bad weather' at a cost of £29 19s 9d. Both the Tower and the Gibbon ropeworks were acquired though at different periods, the former by Messrs Catto, subsequently Catto & Thomson (in which Alexander Hall & Co. were partners to their cost), the latter by the shipbuilders Walter Hood & Co., then both were taken over by Duthie Brothers. In more recent times, Seggie & Co., well known local coal merchants, had a store on the site of the old ropeworks.

John Catto probaby gave his name to Catto Square a heavily populated area between Baltic Street and Garvock Wynd. As well as the ropeworks, he

St Clement Street looking towards Baltic Place. The handsome tenement on the Garvock Wynd corner has been demolished

132

owned a timber yard on land originally referred to as the 'horse barracks' and a mystery surrounds the locus. It was in the York Street area, but where? The lease was originally rouped to Catto in 1803 as part of the 'Stables on the Road to Pocra....sometime ago created for the accomodation of the Cavalry' though whose cavalry I have been unable to ascertain. Materials of the stables were also rouped in 1803, so the cavalry's departure may have been relatively recent. In further roups of 1819 and 1822 the horse barracks are also now described as Catto's timber yard. The list of shoreporters' tariffs may provide a clue to their whereabouts. In the early nineteenth century one of their routes ran 'from the Lower Quays to the Street passing from the Tide betwixt John Rae and James Gibbon's Dock Yards into the Links called Barrack-St'. Rae's yard as shown on page 140, abutted on to York Place which fits the 'Barrack Street' description, running as it does from Waterloo Quay to the Links. And there were certainly timber yards at the junction of York Place and York Street, the later site of Hall Russell's boiler shop. That could have been the old site of these mysterious Cavalry stables.

In 1974 the area south of Cotton Street was declared unsuitable for residential use and the old tenements cleared. I have walked many times from Castle Terrace to the Squares where so many once wrought, without meeting a single soul. Industry has been encouraged to locate in the Upper Fittie area and the Miller Street Industrial Estate is bland and attractively landscaped. A number of transport firms have also acquired premises in the area and I have been alarmed at the number of huge lorries which now rattle at speed along Miller Street and St Clement Street. These narrow, winding streets, the successors of the old Futty Gate are not adequate for such use.

It would be splendid to see these wastelands of Upper Fittie re-zoned again for residential use, where houses, built in the vernacular style, would line genuine streets, ideally placed for the city centre and beach. The problem lies in the fact that the soil has been contaminated after generations of industrial usage. But if oil can be taken from the hostile environment of the North Sea, it is surely within man's capabilites to cleanse a few acres of soil.

Part Four

Shipbuilders and Shipyards

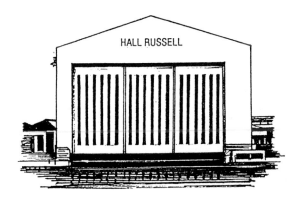

The covered construction hall of 1982

Chapter 12

Early Shipbuilders

For the early shipbuilder, a handshake was as binding as a written contract.

Recollections of an Old Lawyer. Lachlan Mackinnon, 1935.

The history of shipbuilding in Aberdeen began in 1606, not at Footdee, but within the former churchyard of the Trinity Friars, then conveniently lapped by the Denburn estuary at what is now the foot of Guild Street. The magistrates had granted permission to Alexander Davidson, a St Andrew's timber merchant, to build a barque and the Wood of Drum, bought for the purpose, was floated down the Dee. Although it was possible to launch a vessel from the churchyard at high tide, winning to the open sea must have been hazardous in view of the shallow, treacherous nature of the estuary. The fishers' haven at the Pockraw which was close to the harbour mouth and enjoyed a reasonable depth of water was a more sensible choice. No more was heard of the churchyard-dockyard after the first launch, and by the time Parson Gordon was making notes for his *Description of Both Towns of Aberdeen* in the 1650s, he was able to record of Footdee: 'Before it ships doe ly, and lykewayes heir is a docke for building or repairing ships'. This dock appears clearly in Taylor's Plan of 1773, just south-east of the village and at the west end of the Pockraw as shown on page 8.

Although the Gibbon family was among the port's earliest shipbuilders, their yard was initially established in Torry. They later crossed to Footdee. An Arthur Gibbon is recorded as having repaired a fishing boat for £20 Scots in the 1720s but the location is uncertain. The best known of Footdee's early shipbuilders, however, was Simon Holliday who had served his apprentice-ship at Deptford, then came north to build a 'barge' for a Captain Strachan of

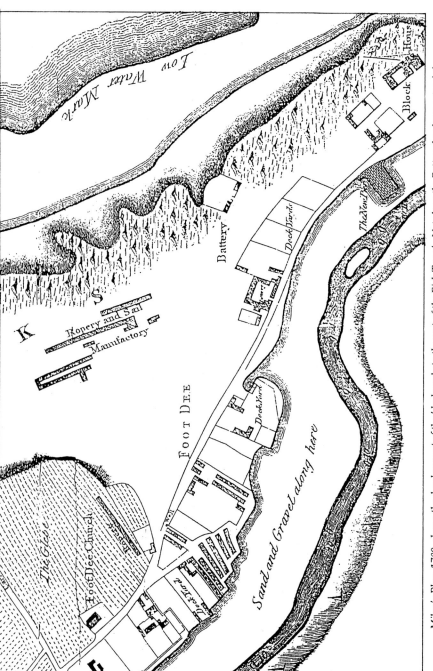

Milne's Plan, 1789, shows the development of the 'dockyards to the east of the Fish Town'. Note how the Pottery has been extended.

Aberdeen. In 1753, according to the burgh records, he leased a piece of open ground at the south-east end of Footdee, one hundred yards by thirty yards, to be enclosed both as a woodyard and as a dock for repairing ships. Judging by the date and the description, this appears to be the same dockyard as shown in Taylor's Plan. Here Holliday lauched, 'a fine new vessel....the first of the kind ever built in this Place'. It seems that he ran his business in a hand-to-mouth style. In 1753, the Town Council voted him £60 sterling for a dwelling house, but timber for his next vessel had already arrived in port, the freight, £40 sterling, payable on delivery. Holliday solved the problem of lack of ready cash by petitioning the magistrates for the immediate payment of the £60 earmarked for the house.

The dockyard itself had become a landmark in the area. In September 1758 the Justice Court Book recorded the cases of three women delated (charged) with fornication and adultery. The alleged partner of one of the three firmly denied the charge despite circumstantial evidence brought by Margery Burnett of their assignation in 'the southmost house of Futtie next to the shipbuilders'.

The demand for vessels to serve the growing trade of the port was such that by 1764 Holliday was unable to keep pace. There was a particular need for lighters to ferry cargo and passengers from vessels anchored in deep water at Fittie, Torry or in the Gawpool to the Town's Quay at the Shiprow. This at least was the argument put forward to the magistrates by two ship carpenters, James Bruce and James Jaffray. They too were permitted to construct a small dockyard 'on the northeast side of the road leading to the new quay at Pocra'. A James Jaffray, a former apprentice of Holliday' s had been press-ganged in 1757, so this could well have been the same man, returned now to compete with his old master.

At this time Holliday himself was prominent in the Footdee Society of which he had been a founder member in 1761, noted in the roll as 'Simon Holyday, carpenter' and paying an entry fee of 10/-. He was unanimously elected Master of the Society two years later and had to deal with the bad behaviour of the clerk James Taylor 'who upon too many occasions comes to the meeting concerned with liquor and incapable to act in the station of clerk'. Taylor was duly 'paid off'. Holliday's signature - that is how he spelt his name while the clerk preferred Holyday - was, with that of a successor, James Abernethy, probably the most distinctive in the Minute Book.

In 1767 Holliday requested the magistrates for a twenty-six year extension of his lease, indicating that he was anxious to erect new buildings and a sawmill at a cost of some £200. The lease was duly extended, but for reasons unknown, he renounced it soon afterwards, disposing of his house and dockyard for 100 guineas. At the time of applying for the lease, Holliday had expressed misgivings about undertaking improvements when all would revert to the Town on his death, so perhaps he had second thoughts. A twenty-

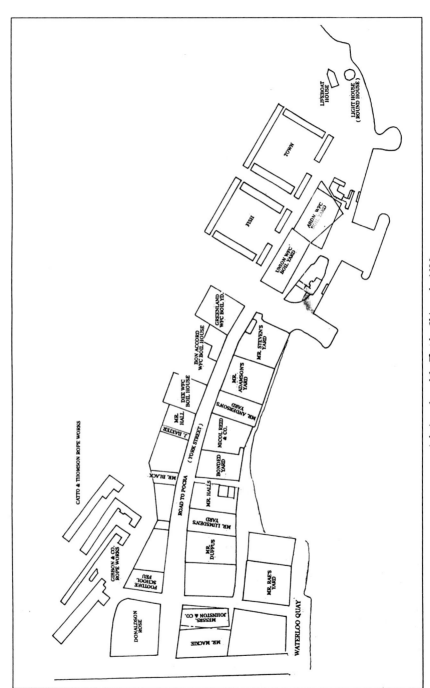

A feuing plan of the Footdee Shipyards, 1820

three year tack (lease) of the dockyard was subsequently granted to Walter McKail.

Holliday's house was one of those substantial Footdee dwellings of which tantalising glimpses are afforded down the years. A later owner was Edward Rae, well known in his time as a Fittie shipbuilder and timber merchant, and by 1837 it had become the Victoria Tavern, regarded then as 'an old house of somewhat peculiar construction'. In 1840 it went up in flames with the loss of five lives, a tragedy long-remembered in the area.

By the 1780s shipbuilding was booming in Fittie and the magistrates appointed a Committee to receive petitions from potential shipbuilders wishing to lease dockyards. In 1788 five sites were available on the Road leading to Pocra, fronting on to the fishers' haven. Milne's Plan of 1789, on page 138, makes an interesting comparison with Taylor's Plan on page 8, showing how the shipyards had expanded in the intervening sixteen years. The Pottery appears about to be swallowed up and its fate is the subject of speculation in the next chapter. Milne also shows a dockyard on the Aberdeen side of Fittie, but that would have been a less convenient site.

In the decade or so between 1787 and 1799 ninety-five vessels were built, and in 1818 Kennedy reported that twenty-two had been launched during the preceding year. 'There are upwards of six building yards, in constant employment, either in building new vessels, or in repairing old ones'. Nor were these limited to small ships for the coasting trade. As Kennedy commented: 'One of the vessels called the *Castle Forbes* lately launched is intended for the trade to India, and is the first ship built at Aberdeen for that purpose.' A feuing plan of 1820, opposite, shows a dozen yards: 'Mr J. Duffus, Mr Lumsdens yard, Mr Halls, Nicol Reid & Co. Mr Anderson's Yard, Mr Adamsons Yard and Mr Stevens Yard,' the latter being at the south-east end, near the present Footdee bus terminus. We can hope that his premises had improved since 1788 when he requested the magistrates for permission to erect props outside the dockyard fence to support the stern of a vessel he was building.

William Stephen (that is the usual spelling) was a renowned ship draughtsman and Provost Daniel Mearns recalled that he had seen a receipt dated 1787 in acknowledgement of £3 paid by James Cochar, the father-in-law of Alexander Hall to Stephen for instruction. Stephen also had a timber yard on the north side of York Street, and appears to have owned land nearby in what by 1816 had become Wellington Street. The earliest document relating to No 57, one of the few older properties still extant in industrial Footdee, shows that title to the land on which the house was built passed in 1817 from William Stephen to Alexander Gibbon, Duncan Davidson, proprietor of Inchmarlo, Banchory, and Robert Pirie, all of whom were much involved in harbour business. In 1828 the firm of William Stephen & Sons was taken over by one of his sons and relocated on Clydeside where it became world famous as Alexander Stephen & Sons, Linthouse.

Another well known early shipbuilder was John Duffus whom we have already briefly met. He was closely involved with the firm which became the Aberdeen Steam Navigation Company and in 1827 Duffus & Co. launched Aberdeen's first paddle-steamer, *Queen of Scotland*, for Aberdeen Steam's London run thus, ironically, triggering off Footdee's great era of clipper building as will be discovered. The *Queen,* with two engines of seventy-five horse power was 'calculated to carry, besides her machinery, fuel etc. three hundred tons'. Apart from luxuries such as 'two splendid cabins', she converted to a gunboat at the drop of a hat, or at least the removal of her stanchions. At her launch, Duffus's competitors in the neighbouring yards public spiritedly opened their premises to accommodate the great crowds that cheered her down the slips, albeit in pouring rain.

Queen of Scotland almost came a cropper on her first trial on August 25, 1827. Work on her engines was so far behind that 120 mechanics had to be taken on board to continue their labours. It was an eventful trip for them. A fire broke out around midnight which they helped to put out. Then high winds made it impossible for them to land until the following afternoon. Little damage was done, however, and the *Queen* was soon afterwards placed on the regular London run. John Duffus & Co., built four further London Boats for Aberdeen Steam, the *Duke of Wellington, North Star, City of Aberdeen* and the ill-fated *Duke of Sutherland.*

Queen of Scotland, Aberdeen's first paddle steamer.

142

The Queen of Scotland's engines and boilers were constructed 'in-house' at Duffus's nearby Footdee Iron Works on the old glebe of St Clement's Kirk, running from Garvock Wynd to Links Street where the firm's extensive ropeworks stretched back to the Links. Duffus advertised the works for sale in 1841, stressing their extensive equipment; blacksmiths, millwrights, engineering and boiler shops, a foundry, a timber yard, a warehouse, a porter's lodge and 'an excellent Dwelling-house for a Manager'. In fact John Duffus merged with Blaikie Brothers, Ironfounders, four years later on the same site. The latter firm added 'Millwrights and Mechanics' to the impressive list of services previously offered by John Duffus.

The Blaikie Brothers, sons of the John Blaikie who carried on a flourishing business as plumber and brassfounder in Littlejohn Street were high fliers rather than 'rude mechanicks'. James Blaikie of Craigiebuckler, Advcocate in Aberdeen, was Provost from 1833-35 and shares the distinction with his Grammar School classmate, Lord Byron, of a splendid statue in his memory. Not to be outdone, a younger brother, Sir Thomas Blaikie, Provost in 1839-46 and 1853-55 has his Quay. A third brother, David, lived at Balgownie Lodge, and a fourth, John, at Devanha House, Ferryhill. A fifth, Patrick became acquainted with Napoleon, but that is another story....

John, Thomas and David were the founding partners of Blaikie Brothers and they launched the iron brig *Centaur* in 1847. From 1878 until its demise in 1891 the firm built engines for John Duthie's trawlers. Blaikie Brothers were nothing if not versatile, carrying on for many years 'an enormous business' throughout the country as bridge builders including many railway bridges, particularly on the Deeside Line. Thomas was Chairman of the Deeside Railway Board. The bridge that crossed the line at Pittengullies, Peterculter for example bore the plaque: 'Built by Blaikie Bros, Engineers, Footdee, 1882'. They also diversified into coffee and sugar mills and Lachlan Mackinnon recalling the last days of the company in his *Recollections of an Old Lawyer* (1935) noted that:

> When a consigment was despatched, the mills formed an impressive parade in Union Street as they followed each other in a long train of horse-drawn vehicles. The firm fell on evil times towards the end of last century, and one of the managers who had an old West India connection was sent there to get orders. But beet sugar had killed the enterprise in cane sugar, and the only order brought back was for a set of tomb railings - appropriate to enclose the grave of still-born expectations.

In 1900, the former Blaikie Brothers premises were taken over by the timber firm of John Fleming & Co. Ltd. as already noted, and the area was named Baltic Place.

Another early firm, Vernon Bowman alias Bowman Vernon and even John Vernon & Sons had the distinction of building Aberdeen's first iron ship the

John Garrow in 1837. Three years later she created a sensation as the first iron ship on the Tyne. There appears to have been no room for Vernon Bowman on the prime York Street site fronting the old fishers' haven, so in 1837 the firm leased the former Davis Straits/Greenland Whale Fishing Company boilyard on the opposite side of York Street across from William Stephen's old yard. These premises, the Dee Iron Works, faced out to sea and strict instructions were issued by the Commissioners of the Northern Lights that no light should be allowed to escape. Confusion to mariners was obviously anticipated, given that Girdleness Lighthouse operational since 1833 was only a mile east as the crow, or perhaps the seagull flies. Vernon's old premises were later occupied by Messrs John Rust & Co. timber merchants.

William Simpson, Blacksmith, is noted in the Shoremaster's Accounts in the 1790s, and he is probably be the same William Simpson whose York Place Iron Works remained operational from the late eighteenth century until the early 1850s. Simpson was a founding father of industrial Footdee and a forebear of Lord Provost Daniel Mearns who paid tribute to him in a lecture at St Clement's Church in 1896 published that year in the Futtie Kirk Bazaar Book. 'Although I never saw him,' Mearns said, 'I have heard a good deal of his energy and pluck, and although he did not live to an old age, he left proof of his ability to organise.' And he continued:

William Simpson, along with several others, started the firm which for so long bore his name....Of course it was not a shipbuilding firm then, but it did a great deal of shipbuilding work. They were, in those early days, blacksmiths, chainmakers, anchor-makers, moulders and a great many things too numerous to mention. He also helped the starting of the ropeworks, the block-making, and pump-making, in short, all description of material used by ships. He took an interest in the development of the coasting trade to London, also the developing of the Baltic trade in hemp and flax yarn. In this he was assisted by the Messrs Catto and other well-known citizens..... He did not however live to see any of the fruits of his labour.

In 1837 a piece of ground owned by Alexander Mackie Jnr, doubtless a scion of the land-owning Mackies

Lord Provost Daniel Mearns.

144

discussed in Chapter 3, was rouped to William Simpson & Co., Blacksmiths. William Simpson, already in possession of ground nearby, expanded his York Place Iron Works. The building still stands, bounded by York Street, St Clement Street, Wellington Street and York Place, battered, grimy, still in use, and one of the most interesting pieces of industrial archaeology in Aberdeen. William Simpson began to supply engines for vessels built by the nearby firm of Alexander Hall & Co., at the very time that Halls were also building their epoch-making clippers, an indication of the versatility of this renowned firm. During the decade up to 1850, for example, Simpson & Co. supplied the engines for four Hall vessels commencing in 1840 with those for the schooner-

Charles Mitchell.

rigged, steam-propelled *Gazelle* which came off Halls' stocks immediately after their clipper *Scottish Maid* with her prototype Aberdeen Bow.

Among William Simpson's employees was John Coutts, son of an Aberdeenshire farmer who later moved to Bowman, Vernon & Co., and helped to design the *John Garrow*. Another was the apprentice draughtsman Charles Mitchell who took first prize in chemistry at the Marischal College evening classes in 1840 which at that time included physics and other subjects relevant to the forward-looking shipbuilder. In his spare time Mitchell also gave lessons in ship draughting to Andrew Leslie, foreman boilermaker with Bowman Vernon. Indeed Footdee suffered a brain drain in the early 1840s when Coutts, Vernon, Leslie and Mitchell all moved to Tyneside and subsequently established shipyards that were all famous in their day. Coutts is credited with building the first major iron ship on the Tyne.

In the early 1860s Mitchell's firm built several large warships for the Russian Navy at the time when Alexander Hall & Co. was virtually creating the Japanese Navy. So if the ensuing Russo-Japanese War can be seen as something of a Mitchells v. Halls contest, Halls were the winners. (I hasten to add the comparison is somewhat spurious!) Charles Mitchell is one of Aberdeen University's greatest benefactors, funding in the 1890s to the tune of £33,000, the Anatomy Department, the Students' Union, the Mitchell Hall and the Mitchell Tower which are named in his honour. He received the LL.D of Aberdeen University in 1893 but his death two years later deprived him of receiving the Freedom of the City and attending the opening of the Mitchell Hall. His son, Charles W. Mitchell generously took on his father's mantle and made further benefactions.

Back in Fittie, Simpson's York Place Iron Works 'within 100 yards of the Dock' and 'capable of turning out.....the largest size of Marine and Land engines, Locomotive Engines, Railway Furnishings and General Machinery and Blacksmith Work' had been offered for sale as a going concern in 1849 at the reduced upset price of £10,000. They were to be rouped at the Lemon Tree tavern on December 12 and the advertisement in the *Aberdeen Journal* of the previous week was addressed to 'Engineers, Machine-Makers, Boiler-Makers, Steam-ship and Locomotive Builders'. There is an interesting description of the works, which included Turning, Fitting-up and Finishing Shops, Millwrights and Pattern Shops, a large Iron Foundry, a Brass Foundry; Forging and Blacksmiths' Shops, a Boiler Shop, Iron Store, Warehouses and a Counting House. 'The whole of the buildings are in excellent order, having been erected only ten years ago at a large expense', the advertisement continues. 'Some of the locomotive tools are quite new and are capable of turining out every kind of iron work including the largest size of marine and land engines'. And the advertisement goes on to give a picture of the industrial Aberdeen of this era:

The demand for Machinery and Iron goods is very extensive in this city....and the large and increasing number of steam vessels engaged in the trade of the port, together with the Railway communication about completed to the south must very greatly augment that demand, and consequently add to the value of these works.

One cannot help but wonder why Simpson & Co. were selling up. It sounds as though the firm had overreached itself. It continued under the same name for some further years, however, though there were various changes of partnership. Simpson & Co. eventually vanished from the street directory in 1854 and the works stood empty for a considerable time which was not uncommon in Footdee. In 1863 a new company, Hall Russell & Co. acquired and modernised the premises but that is another story.

Chapter 13

Alexander Hall & Co

My grandfather was a shipbuilder in Aberdeen as early as 1780. My father joined
him in business about 1785.
William Hall at the sequestration of Alex Hall & Co. January, 1870

Alexander Hall, a farmer's son from Auchterless in Aberdeenshire, and a
cartwright and ploughwright to trade, came to Footdee in 1785 at the age of
twenty-five to try his luck as a ship carpenter. He was employed by the
shipbuilder Alexander Gibbon, a member of the ubiquitous harbour family
and must have excelled at his work. By 1790 he was taken into partnership
with Gibbon and James Cochar, a ship draughtsman who some years before
had been trained by one of Footdee's early shipbuilders, William Stephen.
Hall and Gibbon are indicated as neighbouring proprietors in the Footdee
quarter in the city Rent Rolls of 1795. James Cochar had died by this time, and
his widow is shown as a tenant of Gibbon's. By 1801, however, Widow Cochar
had become a proprietor in her own right and Alexander Hall had married her
daughter Elizabeth, sixteen years his junior. Of their seven children, who
survived into adulthood, two sons, James and William would succeed their
father as shipbuilders. Hall had meanwhile entered into partnership with a
shipbuilder called Buchan, but their association was short-lived. By May 1809,
Gibbon too was dead and his dockyards let to 'Hall & Co. Carpenters' at £3.12
yearly.
    Alexander Hall's first ship, the *Glasgow Packet* of 82 tons was launched in
1811 and the firm built three ships that year. One of their earliest orders was
the *Plough*, 86 tons, for William Gray and Alex Mitchell, grain merchants of
Newburgh. In 1813, Hall built the *Inverness and Cromarty Packet* for the
Aberdeen & North Shipping Co. and another early customer was the Earl of

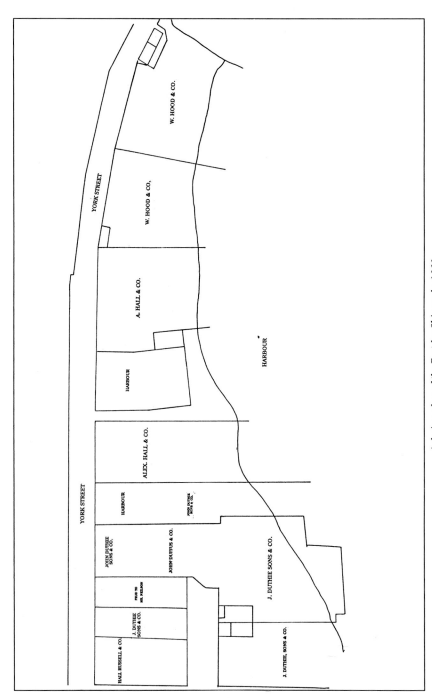

A feuing plan of the Footdee Shipyards, 1866.

Aboyne who ordered two brigs, *Expedition* in 1817 and *Hannah More* in 1819. In 1818, the firm launched the *Asia*, 582 tons, overtaking their *Don*, 332 tons of four years earlier as the largest vessel then built in Aberdeen. People came from miles around to see the launch which went off with great éclat, 'a band discoursing music on board'. Hall & Co. launched Aberdeen harbour's first steam tug in 1827, the *Paul Jones*, at 29 tons their smallest vessel. She acted as unofficial lifeboat for many years

With, to use modern parlance, a full order book for schooners, sloops, smacks and brigantines, Alexexander Hall had been expanding steadily in Fittie over the years. The feuing plan of 1820 on page 140 shows 'Mr Halls' yard centrally placed in the row that fronted onto the fishers' haven. Behind the yards ran the Road to Pocra, soon to become York Street, where Hall was already renting additional ground from the Town Council who owned much of the land in the area. Shipyard leases normally ran for a nineteen year period, and it seems that 'Keep Out' notices and burglar proof premises were as essential in industrial Fit'ie then as now. In 1837 the firm found it necessary to petition the Town Council for permission to erect a 12 ft fence or brick wall since the wooden railing at their yard was 'altogether insufficient both for keeping Depredators out and protecting the Material required in the business of shipbuilding'. Permission to build a wall of quarry pinnings and mortar and lime was granted.

Alexander's sons James and William had taken over in 1835, the former responsible for management, the latter for design, leaving their father, at 75, to enjoy a well earned retirement of some fourteen years. In 1839 the brothers were commissioned by a local consortium to build a fast schooner for the coastal trade to challenge the paddle steamers of the Aberdeen Steam Navigation Company which, thanks to their gigantic fuel consumption, were not cost effective. 'It appears that the model approved by the owners was for a fast schooner with a conventional bow', wrote Hazel Carnegie in *Harnessing the Wind*. But William Hall had, on his own initiative, carried out tank tests, using models of a new hull shape. The design entailed running the stem out so as to form the cutwater, drawing the water lines finer at the bow, and as a natural consequence, the vessel would divide the water easily, and be more buoyant forward. This streamline stem became known as the Aberdeen Bow.

The initial scepticism of the canny Aberdeen consortium, led by Alexander Nicol, merchant, shipowner and Lord Provost from 1866-68, and including the merchant William Hogarth and three paper-making Piries, soon turned to praise and enthusiasm. The little *Scottish Maid*, of 142 tons, contract price £1700, launched in 1839 and placed under the command of 'Old Watson', became the prototype for some of the world's fastest clippers for the Halls generously did not patent their design. 'She was', recalled Danny Mearns, 'the first of the great clippers which raised the name and fame of Aberdeen all over

Scottish Maid, Hall's prototype clipper.

the commercial world'. And unlike Aberdeen's great clippers which generally worked out of London and Liverpool, the *Scottish Maid*, as a coaster, was
frequently to be seen tied up at Provost Blaikie's Quay.

The Aberdeen Bow was later used to great advantage in the construction
of larger vessels and in the decade that followed, of the sixty-four ships built
by Halls only eleven were without it. Of *Scottish Maid's* immediate successors,
the *Glentanar*, 610 tons, built for a Liverpool firm, Yule, Wylie & Co., broke an
unusual record - for speed in construction in 1842. The name came from the
Glentanar estate which had been leased by Hall for shipbuilding. The timber
was cut and floated down the Dee and, 'in six weeks time', wrote Victoria
Clark in *The Port of Aberdeen*, 'the ship was completed, launched, and sped on
her way to America to secure and deliver a cargo of guano before the date fixed
for the imposition of an increased duty'. The *William Punton* which Halls built
the following year for the Newfoundland firm of J Munn & Co. was soon
hailed as 'one of the fastest of Munn's little flyers'.

Fate and genius now combined to bring about Footdee's most brilliant era.
In 1845 Halls built the *Torrington* for the renowned mercantile house of Jardine
Matheson & Co. She was, Danny Mearns noted euphemistically, 'sent to
China to engage in the coasting trade' and caused something of a sensation.
The Lord Provost did not mention that she was an opium runner. Then came
the great tea races. Back in 1842, the Treaty of Nanking had opened Chinese
ports to British trade, followed in 1849 by the repeal of the protectionist British
Navigation Laws. Fast American clippers, built initially for the Californian

150

The Reindeer. Courtesy of Aberdeen Art Gallery and Museums Collection.

gold rush of 1848 began to dominate the China tea trade. The race was on.

The Footdee-built clippers of the Halls and their colleagues, commissioned by British merchants, now challenged the 'Jonathans', as the Americans were known. Halls' small schooner, *Reindeer* 328 tons, commissioned by a Liverpool firm made a record journey to China in 1850, and was the first to arrive with the new teas. Impressed, Jardine Matheson ordered the clipper *Stornoway* from Halls through Captain J Robertson who became her commander. She was custom-built in 1850, specifically to race against the Americans, and beating vessels twice her size. The *Chrysolite*, 440 tons for J R Wardley of Liverpool followed in 1851, overtaking three Yankee racing clippers on the homeward run following her maiden voyage.

American vessels were twice the tonnage of the largest British ships, so Halls speculatively laid down 'a clipper of larger size and finer lines than had been previously built in Scotland'. This vessel of 787 tons with a contract price of £15,434 was purchased by a consortium of David Jardine, Canton China, of Jardine Matheson, and Captains J Robertson of Liverpool and Duncan Forbes of Aberdeen. It appears that Robertson of the *Stornoway* had initially advised his employers that a fine new vessel was under construction at Footdee, and Jardine Matheson decided to offer for her. 'She has been launched under the name of *Cairngorm*, and sailed from Aberdeen on 24 February 1853', commented the *Illustrated London News* ten days later. 'The vessel has been greatly admired by judges as perfect in symmetry and workmanship'. She was not only faster than her 'Jonathan' rivals, but it was said that because of her

A contemporary engraving of The Cairngorm.

superior design she brought home the tea in better condition.

While constructing record-breaking vessels of breathtaking beauty, the Halls continued to be fully involved with developments in Footdee, and with the welfare of local folk. At the time they had the magnificent *Cairngorm* on the stocks, they were also busy repairing 'the Gutta Percha Safety Boat for the Beach'. John Smith, the Town's Superintendent, had constructed a new lifeboat shed but declined responsibility for the boat herself, declaring that to be 'altogether out of his Depth'. James Hall, however, took responsiblity for maintenance, making her like new after being damaged, and guaranteeing that one of his men would 'look at her every Saturday to ascertain her condition during the Season'. In the following year, 1854, James Hall, as already noted, expressed concern to the Council over crowded conditions in the Fisher Squares. And that same year the firm was working on the *Schomberg*, at 2284 tons the largest wooden ship built in Britain to that date and the only one, according to the maritime writer Basil Lubbock, that could in any way compare with the big Boston and Nova Scotia clippers. James Baines of Liverpool had been much impressed by the success of Halls' little tea clippers and had ordered her for his Black Ball passenger line. In *The Colonial Clippers*, Lubbock commented:

She had three skins, two of diagonal planking, and one fore and aft, the whole fastened together with screw-threaded hard-wood trunnels - a novelty in shipbuilding. She was specially heavily rigged, her mainmast weighing 15 tons, being a pitch-pine spar 110 feet in length and 42 inches in diameter.

Unfortunately her master, James 'Bully' Forbes, an Aberdonian and 'a most resolute man, absolutely fearless, of quick decision, but of mercurial temperament' managed to lose her on her maiden voyage to Australia. He is reported as having remained below playing whist, ignoring all warnings while *Schomberg* settled on a sandbank and eventually broke up. Halls at that time had no experience in building massive emigrant clippers, and it was thought that Bully Forbes, frustrated at the slowness of the passage, had allowed her to ground on purpose. This episode, not surprisingly, ended his career with the Black Ball Line.

Schomberg had initially set off for Australia in fine fettle with flags flying and bands playing. Conversely, twelve years on, Halls' *Sobraon* of 2131 tons had the worst of baptisms for her owners were in financial difficulties and unable to accept delivery. They arranged a resale and she became one of Devitt & Moore's regular packets to Australia, though Halls lost £4000 on the deal. But how different the subsequent fate of the two vessels. *Sobraon*, the largest composite ship ever built and 'one of the finest passenger sailing ships ever launched' was constructed of finest Malabar teak, with beams of iron. Passengers specifically booked aboard *Sobraon* because of the high reputation of her commander, Captain J A Elmslie, the kindly disciplinarian with his 'never ceasing attention to the ship and the weather'. Most telling of all, her ship's company was something of a permanent fixture. James Cameron, foreman shipwright at Footdee not only built her but sailed with her as carpenter from 1866-1891, her entire life afloat. She was then bought by the government of New South Wales as a reformatory ship and in 1911, still 'as sound as a bell', was converted into a training ship for the Australian Navy.

During the 1850s Halls built over three dozen clippers and schooners and adapted the small screw yacht *Fox* for Captain Leopold McClintock's successful Arctic search for the remains of the Franklin expedition as well as *Artisa* and *Agricola* for the Northern Agricultural Company which had recently set up in business at Waterloo Quay. In the 1860s came another batch of 'China Run' clippers, *Flying Spur*, *Black Prince*, *Fuchow*, and *Yangtse*, winner of the 1867 tea race under the fearless Captain Kemball.

Halls also founded the Japanese Navy. In 1859 the entrepreneurial trader, Thomas Blake Glover, a son of the coastguard at the Bridge of Don, arrived in Nagasaki at a time when Japan was re-entering the international scene after more than two centuries isolation. His elder brothers, Charles and James, had set up in Aberdeen as shipbrokers, trading from No 47, and later from No 19 Marischal Street and through them Thomas ordered a famous series of warships from Halls and later Hall Russell for his Japanese contacts. In 1868 Thomas Glover commissioned a gunboat for the warring Choshu clan from Halls, the barque-rigged screw steamer *Ho Sho Maru* with engines by Hall Russell.

The following year he ordered a twelve gun corvette again from Halls, the *Jho Sho Maru* of 1459 tons, rigged for steam or sail, and destined for another warring faction, the Higo clan. Fitting out, including the application of a belt of armour plating on the waterline was carried out, as was the usual practice, near the dock gates, alongside George Milne's timber yard across on Blaikie's Quay. Disaster struck when the *Jho Sho Maru* was almost ready to sail for Japan. Fire broke out in Milne's yard. James Hall rushed to the scene, giving orders that the warship be pulled into the middle of Victoria Dock, out of harm's way. He crossed to the woodyard, not without difficulty for the dock gates were closed, and was leading the firefighting team when flames burst through the floor at his feet and he suffered a fatal heart attack. The ship was saved but James Hall's death cast a gloom over Footdee.

To complete the Japanese saga, by the time the *Jho Sho Maru* reached Japan, the country was at peace. The two Hall warships, and a third, the Hall Russell-built *Wen Yu Maru*, now formed the Imperial Navy of a united Japan. *Jho Sho Maru* had been offered to the Emperor Meiji by the Higo clan and became his 'imperial vessel'. Alexander McKay, an authority on Thomas Glover, notes that within ten years, the Japanese Navy had expanded from 'a few small inshore vessels to three state-of-the-art deep sea fighting ships', thanks to the Glovers and the Fittie shipyards. To service the growth of shipping at

The Jho Sho Maru before leaving Aberdeen. Note the Japanese insignia on the bow. Courtesy, Aberdeen Art Gallery and Museums Collections.

154

Nagasaki, a patent slip dock constructed by Hall Russell was shipped to that port in the clipper *Helen Black*, custom-built by Halls in 1868 for that undertaking. And it was during these years Thomas Glover was recognised as one of the founding fathers of modern Japan and was honoured by the Emperor, becoming the first non-Japanese samurai.

While building these warships for the warring Japanese clans, Halls were simultaneously aiding the cause of peace and Christianity, building the missionary ships, *John Williams* (1865) and *Samoa* (1868) for the London Missionary Society. Nor were local interests neglected. In 1869, the year the *Jho Sho Maru* was built, the *May Queen* for Shirras Laing and Leslie of Aberdeen was also launched. In that year too, the *Caliph* (her owner had lived for many years in Bagdad), a composite ship of wooden planking and iron frames was constructed at a cost of £46,032 for Alexander Hector of London, under the

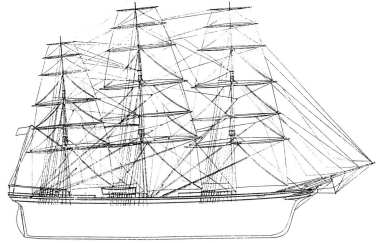

The Caliph.

supervision of William's son. William Jnr was a Marischal College graduate who on serving his apprenticeship at Footdee, sailed round the world to gain experience, a far cry from the days when his ploughwright grandfather arrived in Footdee from Auchterless to seek his fortune. Designed specifically to compete with the *Cutty Sark* and *Thermopylae*, the *Caliph* was hailed as Halls' masterpiece. Captain Henderson, a former master of *Thermopylae*, sailed her from Footdee to London and declared her the fastest ship he ever had anything to do with. However 1869 was to prove Halls' *annus horribilis* and she was to be an unlucky ship. She never had the opportunity to prove herself, vanishing mysteriously in the China Seas in 1871 during her second voyage. As it transpired, she was Halls' and Aberdeen's last tea clipper.

A few months after James Hall's death in June 1869, the company failed. There were several reasons. Alexander Hall & Co. owned 50 per cent of the

*Alexander Hall & Co's staff in 1862. The ships on the stocks are left,
the Coulmakyle and the Natal Star.*

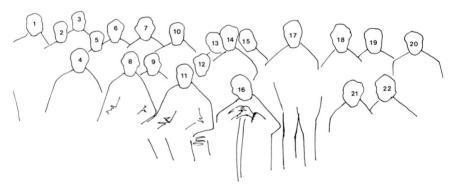

1. A H Wilson, shipbuilder 2. J M Carnie, foreman carpenter 3. Wm Ligertwood, boatbuilder 4. James
Shand, foreman carpenter 5. Alex Guyan, gatekeeper 6. George Sim, carpenter 7. John Hadden,
blockmaker 8. Walter Dinnet, foreman carpenter 9. Robert Robertson, blacksmith 10. James Morrison,
blacksmith 11. James Mitchell, foreman carpenter 12.? 13. Wm Shearer, cashier 14. John Gunn,
foreman carpenter 15. Peter Anderson, foreman joiner 16. James Anderson Jnr, carpenter 17. Wm Hall
18. Alexander Hall Jnr 19. James Hall 20. Wm Goodbrand, carpenter 21. John Cruickshank, office boy
22. Robert Croll, office boy

rope and sailmaking firm, Catto & Thomson, one of whose partners, George Thomson had absconded in 1863 after using the firm's name to obtain personal credit. Halls were liable for half of this debt, some £25,000. Additionally, between 1866 and 1868, the firm lost £4000 on the *Sobraon* as already noted, £1700 on the *Taiwan* which was built speculatively and sailed to China to find a buyer, and even £500 on the *Jho Sho Maru*. James's contract price of £46,032 had been too low. William calculated that losses since Thomson absconded amounted to £36,000 which the firm had struggled for some years to make good. Financial pressures had even caused the brothers to fall out in 1867 when James gave A Hall Wilson, the nephew that he and his wife had brought up, half his shares in Hall Russell. Wilson, a former Halls' apprentice had been assumed into partnership in the new firm but William argued that at such a time it was essential for the brothers to retain what cash they had. By November 1869 the City of Glasgow Bank had stopped credit. For a time William paid wages and bills from an advance on a ship, and with help from a friend. At the end of December, however, he had no option but to apply for sequestration. During a three-day sale the following June, the entire ship-building plant and tools were auctioned, chiefly to Dundee and Glasgow shipbuilders.

There had been much sympathy in Footdee and in Aberdeen for William's bereavement and financial predicament. The Halls were regarded as good employers. They ran evening classes at which their apprentices were tutored, not only in the three Rs, but also in drawing and modelling if they showed aptitude. Like their colleagues in the other Footdee yards, the brothers were always on the scene in person in the event of a shipwreck, ready to offer assistance in these pre-RNLI days. Their shipwrights had formed one of the earliest Co-operative stores in Aberdeen, and their Carpenters' Ball, funded by the apprentices' launch money and held in the drafting loft every Hogmanay, was Footdee's social event of the year. James Hall, along with other Fittie stalwarts, William Duthie, George Thompson, John Gibb and William Hogarth had served on the Committee of the Footdee Dispensary which in the first half of the nineteenth century operated as an early form of NHS industrial practice and was 'particularly beneficial as the means of affording prompt medical aid in cases of accident, which are of frequent occurence amongst those employed at the Shipping, Harbour, and extensive works at Footdee'. Halls also became the first shipyard to inaugurate the Saturday half day.

All was not lost however. After the crash, Alexander Hall & Co. had been left with assets of £67,070 10s as against liabilities of £76,831 and the position was far from hopeless. The business was carried on by a judicial factor and by 1871 William was back at the helm with William Jnr assumed as partner.

The firm was now looking forward again, making the change over to iron, their last wooden vessel leaving the stocks in 1875. A decade later, the clipper age itself was drawing to a close. In 1885 the firm launched the *Torridon* and the *Yalleroi*, their last two clippers for Lord Provost Nicol's Australian wool trade. And it was at the end of the clipper era, in 1887, that William Hall passed away at his home in York Street in his 81st year. In *Recollections of an Old Lawyer*, Lachlan Mackinnon has provided a memorable glimpse of the inventor of the Aberdeen Bow:

> the lady who was to christen the ship did not give sufficient impetus to the bottle and away went the vessel down the ways with the bottle unbroken and dangling at the end of a ribbon ....It would have been a most unlucky thing to let the good ship go into the water unbaptised, but Mr William Hall the builder was equal to the occasion and, though an old man, leapt off the platform and pursued the vessel down the ways until he caught her up, seized the bottle and duly smashed it on her retreating bow. He picked his way back as if he had done nothing unusual though he had run no small risk amid flying timbers and the clanking anchor chains as they ran out.

By the time of William's death, his sons William Jnr and James had been involved in the running of the company for some years. Halls had absorbed the firm of Walter Hood & Co. in 1881 and were able to expand by taking over the former Hood yard at the east end of York Street. The switch from wood

Halls shipyard c1900. By this time the firm had absorbed Walter Hood's yard at the east end of York Street. Courtesy, Aberdeen Art Gallery and Museums Collections.

to iron had been followed by the switch from sail to steam, and the trawler era, coming hard on the heels of the clipper era was now providing the lion's share of orders. Halls' first trawler, the *Maggie Walker* was built for Thomas Walker in 1888. Other customers of those days included W H Dodds of North Shields, George W Bowman of Hull, and the North British Steam Fishing Company. By 1889, the premises occupied nearly five acres on both sides of York Street, and according to the commercial journal *Scotland of Today*, included a large shipyard with engine and boiler works, and a foundry and machine shops, all of which were 'equipped with improved machinery and apparatus of the best modern type'. The journal reported five steamers on the stocks, and noted that the firm exported marine engines and boilers to all parts of the world, as well as supplying the home market. This was an interesting development for in the late 1860s, Halls was still supplying hulls only in joint ventures with Hall Russell who produced the engines.

In 1904, the family connection ended with William Jnr's retirement. The firm became a limited company as Alexander Hall & Co. Ltd. Between the mid 1880s and 1914 Halls built several passenger-cargo vessels in addition to the numerous trawlers and drifters which were to be the company's forte during the First World War. They provided five trawlers and over thirty Ocean Class drifters for service as Admiralty minesweepers, as well as supervising the construction of the latter at twenty-five other shipyards. In the inter-war years the firm specialised in cargo steamers, grab dredgers barges and tugs including a number for the governments of Israel, the Sudan and the USSR. Trawler construction also continued and by 1940,157 had been had completed. During the Second World War, Halls were back at work for the Admiralty, constructing a number of Flower Class corvettes as well as minesweepers and salvage vessels. After 1945 the diesel and motor trawlers superseded the 'Smokey Jo' and Halls' output now included deep sea trawlers for English east coast ports, and in 1947, five for the Icelandic Goverment.

Packets had been among the earliest craft built by Alexander Hall & Co., and ferries were now to be among their last. The *St Rognvald* and the *St Ola* were completed for the North of Scotland Orkney and Shetland Shipping Company in 1951. Four years later the *Explorer* was custom-built for the Scottish Home Department as a deep sea trawler-cum-fisheries research vessel. *Explorer* gave sterling service to the Marine Laboratory at Torry throughout her career, and on decommissioning in 1984 was acquired at a cost of £33,000 by Aberdeen District Council for conversion to an exhibition vessel. At time of writing, however, no permanent berth has been found for her, and her condition gives cause for concern.

The beginning of the end for Halls came in 1953 when the neighbouring concern of Hall Russell acquired a controlling interest. Halls' last ship, No 877 on the list, was the cargo vessel *Santona*, built for the Donaldson Line in 1958

From the Pottery to Waterside

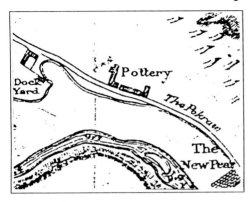

A detail from Taylor's Plan, 1773 showing the Pottery in isolation at the fishers' haven of Pockraw.

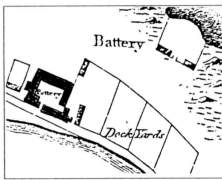

The same area on Milne's plan, 1789. The Pottery has been extended to a square shape and shipyards have appeared on the east side. Note the building on the west of the Pottery, across a gap. ▶

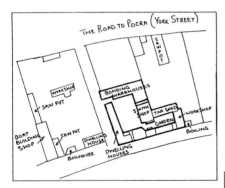

The same square shape appears in the same place on a feuing plan of the area, 1815. It is no longer referred to as the Pottery, but bonded warehouses and a garden on the site indicate a continuing commercial and residential use. A boilhouse is seen near the formerly identified building west of the 'square', noted as a dwelling house, and the gap has become a lane. ◀

Detail from the OS map of 1869 showing the same area. The lane, now clearly seen giving access from York Street is marked "Water-side", the name that now was being applied to the whole 'square' or enclave, completely surrounded by Halls shipyards. ▶
Note Neptune Terrace opposite.

160

and the firms were fully merged the following year. However the plate bearing the name of Alexander Hall & Co. Ltd. was to remain at the entrance to Hall Russell until that firm, in turn, was overtaken by nemesis .

Footnote: The Halls and the Vanishing Pottery.

Brickmaking was carried on at Footdee in the eighteenth century, and numerous deeds relating to Fittie make reference to brick walls and 'privies of brick work'. These bricks were produced at the Pottery, shown on Taylor's Plan of 1773, sitting in isolation at the west end of the fishers' haven. Sixteen years later, Milne's Plan, shows the Pottery apparently about to be engulfed by the new 'dockyards'. These brickworks could well have been out of business by then for Provost Auldjo, owner of the Clayhills near Ferryhill, was supplying bricks for Fittie by the 1790s. But the Pottery had a mix of industrial and residential buildings and families continued to live there. Four families signed the St Clement's Disruption Roll of 1843 giving their address as the Pottery or 'Pottree Close'.

Moreover no less a person than Alexander Hall lived in or near the Pottery, perhaps in the sizeable dwelling immediately to the west in Milne's Plan. 'It was his delight', commented the *Aberdeen Journal* in its obituary of Hall in 1849, 'to join in the sports of the children of the Potterie'. Hall's dwelling may have been the slated house near the Pottery recalled by Ann Allardyce in her memoir of Footdee in the 1780s. It was at that time possessed by an unnamed but affluent shipowner, possibly Captain Arthur Gibbon, but Hall could have acquired it at a later date. The city Rent Rolls of the early nineteenth century show that the Arthur Gibbon, Alexander Hall and his mother-in-law Widow Cochar lived in close proximity. William Skene leaves another clue in his *East Neuk Chronicles* when he recalls a boilhouse 'which would in the present be voted a nuisance' next to Mr Hall's house as late as the 1840s.

In a detail from a feuing plan of the shipyards of *circa* 1815, an enclave in the same position and of the same shape as the Pottery is shown, but now containing bonded warehouses. A lane leading from the Road to Pocra, the future York Street, gives access to the enclave and on the other side is a substantial house with a boilhouse nearby, just as described by Skene. An outline drawing of the same enclave is shown on the feuing plan of 1820 on page 140. And so the vanishing pottery appears to have been absorbed into Halls' yard. Old buildings were useful and it would have been regarded as wasteful to raze them to the ground.

It was probably around 1850 that the former pottery enclave and the lane leading down to it became known as Waterside. In 1853 Messrs Hall & Co requested the Council that the passage from York Street to the Waterside be paved. The Town in fact owned one side of the passage and the Harbour Commissioners the other and was agreed that the two authorities, sometimes at loggerheads, would work together to see what could be done. Indeed in years to come such a demarcation line continued to run through what became Hall Russell's yard.

The first ordnance survey map of Aberdeen of 1869, a detail of which is shown on page 160, shows the same Pottery/Waterside enclave, with the path leading down from York Street noted as Waterside. But by the time this map was published, the shipyards were taking over and the buildings of Waterside alias the Pottery are already being dismantled. In 1862 Halls had applied to the magistrates for permission to remove 'an Old House which abuts into their Building Yard'. Other houses remained in use for a time. The Hall Russell partners met in 'A Hall Wilson's house, Waterside', in 1869, and a little later in 'Mr Wilson's old house in the yard'. This house may also have been known as 'James Hall's House' and its origins may have gone even futher back. It was latterly used as offices before the new York Street block was built on the north side of that road.

Waterside featured briefly in the street directory, making its first appearance in 1871-72 with A Hall Wilson, shipbuilder as the sole occupant. Its last entry a decade later notes it as being opposite 35 York Street. One of

Waterside - or 'Pottree Close"? Note the cottages on the shore and the Whalebone arches. To the rear are warehouses. Left, the horse stands at the foot of Waterside Lane, which gave access from York Street.

Waterside's occupants, James McHardy is described as a draughtsman, doubtless at the shipyard, while another, Miss Allan, was a 'fish merchant at the 'Wet Fish Market'. The Halls themselves had gone west. It was no longer the thing to live over the shop. The small Ruthrieston mansion of Fordbank (later the Park Hotel) had been designed for William Hall Jnr by the distinguished architectural firm of Matthews and Mackenzie in the 1880s. By the turn of the century Waterside had vanished completely, absorbed within the shipyard and in 1982 Hall Russell erected a massive covered building shed near where Waterside had been.

The only memory that remains of Waterside is the photograph opposite, the original of which belonged to the Hall family.

John Duthie, Sons & Co.,
LIMITED,
Shipbuilders,
York Place, Aberdeen.

WILLIAM DUTHIE,
Originator of the firm.
(during the reign of George III.)

JOHN DUTHIE,
from whom firm derived its name
in 1861,
and younger brother of
William Duthie.

ROBERT DUTHIE, son of
John Duthie, Director of
John Duthie, Sons & Co.,
Limited.

WM. JOHNSON, Secretary.

JOHN A. DUTHIE,
son of Robert Duthie, Managing
Director.

Portraits of the Duthie shipowners. Courtesy of Aberdeen Art Gallery and Museums Collections.

Chapter 14

The Duthies and Walter Hood

The world famous Thermopylae was rigged and fitted out, as all the Thompson
clippers were, in the south east corner of the Victoria Dock. These ships seldom
returned to their natal port and I did not see Thermopylae again.

Recollections of an Old Lawyer, Lachlan Mackinnon, 1935.

Among Alexander Hall & Co's more remarkable apprentices were William,
John and Alexander Duthie, sons of a Stonehaven shipmaster, and founders
of a brilliant though confusing shipbuilding dynasty. The first Duthie ship, so
the story goes, was built in Halls' yard in the evenings during 1815, when
Alexander Hall gave his foreman carpenter, William Duthie, the use of empty
stocks. A year later, William had his own shipyard at Footdee and his first
ship was the brigantine *Stranger* which traded between Aberdeen and London, London and Tenerife.

Danny Mearns recalled William not only as a shipbuilder, but as 'a large
timber merchant', trading with North America, Peru (for guano) and Archangel. 'He was about the first shipowner to establish regular traders between
London and Australia'. William Duthie & Co. operated between 1816 and
1837, then William handed the business over to his brothers Alexander and
John, both shipmasters, and to John's son, John Jnr. From 1838 to 1860, the firm
traded as Alexander Duthie & Co. After William's death in 1861 there was a
further reorganisation. Alexander and John Jnr resigned, and John Snr, and
three of his six sons, Alexander, Robert and George became partners in John
Duthie, Sons & Co., the best known of the various permutations of the firm's
name. Their yard in York Place next to the dock gates had berths for four
vessels and a patent slip for ship repairs which in later years was to become an
increasingly important part of the business.

165

Like the Halls, the Duthies were very much a Footdee clan. In the 1830s they lived a stone's throw from head office in York Place. William's home was at 30 St Clement Street, while Alexander's was on Waterloo Quay where he lived with his widowed mother, Mrs Duthie formerly of Stonehaven. John lived in Wellington Street, facing York Street and John Jnr at 27 York Place, that fine neo-classical block designed by John Smith, where a rival shipbuilder, Walter Hood, also had apartments. William and John Snr were great benefactors of St Clement's Kirk, and of the kindly sixteen stone John, Danny Mearns said: 'His happy honest countenance was a sight in itself....many a poor craitur's rent in the district was paid by him, and nobody was the wiser of it'.

During the era of William Duthie & Co. between 1816 and 1837, around seventy vessels were built for local owners; sloops, smacks, schooners, snows, barques and brigantines. They mostly undertook coastal work and the Duthies usually had a share along with other Footdee concerns - the ropemakers Catto Thomson & Co., the shipowners Donaldson Rose & Co. and George Thompson & Co., whose principal we last met in 1848 on Waterloo Quay with the silver keys of the city in his hand, ready to welcome Queen Victoria ashore.

It was between the 1840s and the early 1870s that the Duthies built their world famous clippers. From Alexander's yard came the *Brilliant* of 1850 which carried immigrants to Australia at the time of the gold rush and brought wool home, though *James Booth,* launched the following year, was specifically designed for Booth & Co.'s Calcutta trade. The *Ballarat* of 1852 made a splendid sixty-four day run from London to Sydney, one of the fastest on record. From John Duthie Sons in the 1860s a series of wooden wool clippers all with the Aberdeen Bow, all called after members of the family; the *William Duthie* in 1862, the *Martha Birnie* the following year and the *John Duthie* in 1864, whose commander, Captain Levi was said to offer a glass of Scotch and an apple to any visitor that came aboard. The *Alexander Duthie* followed in 1867, and the *Ann Duthie,* said to have beaten the *Cutty Sark* twice, in 1868. The *Abergeldie* which had iron beams, and the *Windsor Castle* built for Donaldson Rose were both launched in 1869.

Many Duthie ships as their names indicated, were part or wholly owned by the family and some captained by the Duthies. Most traded to Australia, some to China, while the *Peter Denny,* largely owned by the well known Dumbarton shipbuilder and 'a very comfortable happy ship' traded to New Zealand. George Washington Wilson, photographer to Queen Victoria and much of Aberdeen society had a 2/64th share in the *Ann Duthie* and in the *Cairnbulg.* This iron clipper of 1874 traded to Sydney and was was named after the Buchan estate purchased after William's death and entailed in favour of John Snr and his heirs male. Old John remained faithful to Fittie, however, and it was his son John Jnr who became the first Duthie laird of Cairnbulg.

Of John Snr's three sons now in the business, Alexander had spent his younger days as a master of Duthie ships, romantically marrying one of his passengers on the *British Merchant* of 1857, en route for Australia, though her fiancé, awaiting her on the quay at Sydney was none too pleased. Alexander later designed the four-masted iron wool clipper, *Port Jackson*, built under his supervision by Alexander Hall & Co. This seems to have ocasioned something of a family split. In July 1884 a curious notice from the firm of John Duthie Sons & Co. appeared in the *Aberdeen Journal*, pointing out that a recent advertisement had given the erroneous impression that the *Port Jackson* belonged to a firm of old standing. However, the notice continued, 'the firm of Messrs W A and J Duthie was formed within the last two years and owns the *Port Jackson* only. The firm of John Duthie Sons & Co. has been well known in the Aberdeen Trade for quarter of a century, but that is quite a different thing'. Messrs W A and J Duthie were clearly regarded as upstarts by the old brigade. The whole family, however, could have been proud of the *Port Jackson*. 'She was unusually strong and in every way made as perfect as possible', wrote Basil Lubbock. 'She did some very fine performances, notably a run of thirty-nine days from Sydney to San Francisco when she was only three days behind the time of a mail steamer'. She later served as a training ship but went to the bottom in 1917, torpedoed by a German submarine. Aberdeen Maritime Museum has some splendid photographs of her. Of John Snr's other two sons in the business, Robert was also an outstanding clipper designer, while George showed great promise, but died young.

Of the three remaining Duthie sons, John Jnr had not been idle since quitting the shipbuilding firm. He acquired the ropemakers, Catto Thomson & Co. in 1869, doubtless to the relief of William Hall, as well as the neighbouring Walter Hood Ropery on the Links and amalgamated them as Duthie Brothers Rope and Twine Manufacturers and Sail Makers. 'One large and commodious manufactory is spread over four acres with four ropewalks, each over 1000 feet long', the industrial review, *Scotland of Today* reported in 1889, adding rather splendidly, 'Messrs Duthie have lately opened a branch office in London'. Brother James commanded the very fast clipper *Rifleman* (1860) owned by four of the Duthies and George Thompson. James took over management of the Ropery when he returned to dry land. The sixth brother, William, builder of the *Rifleman*, had served apprenticeships both as shipbuilder and shipmaster, and with several other of his brothers was also a partner in the Ropery. He had settled down to run his own shipyard in 1855, initially in Montrose with one of the Cochar family, and from 1856 to 1870 as William Duthie Jnr & Co. His yard was across from Fittie, on the Inches and so outwith our story.

But times were changing and there is a Janus touch about John Duthie in the later nineteenth century. In 1872 the firm completed its first iron screw steamer, the *Lochnagar*, for the Adam shipowning family of Aberdeen. Four

The patent slip at the Duthie yard at the west end of York Street.
Courtesy , Aberdeen Art Gallery and Museums Collections.

years later Duthie launched the *Alexander Nicol* for the Aberdeen Lime Company. But as late as 1877 came one of their finest ships, the family-owned *Brilliant*, the second of that name, which sailed to Australia with general cargo and brought wool home. In *The Colonial Clippers* Basil Lubbock wrote:

> *Brilliant* was a specially handsome ship; painted black with a white under-body, and with a brass rail along the whole length of her topgallant bulwarks, she was always the acme of smartness, being known in Sydney as 'Duthie's Yacht'.

In 1883 a new era began. John Duthie Sons built Aberdeen's first trawler, the *North Star* for William Pyper & Co., with engines by Hall Russell. She was followed by sister ships the *North City* and the *North Cape*, both with engines by Blaikie Brothers. A series of 'Sun' trawlers, *Sunrise*, being the first, was built for Johnstone & Sherrett of Aberdeen between 1891 and 1894. And there were many more. Between 1883 and 1907 when they merged with Hall Russell, Duthies launched over a dozen steam drifters and ninety-four coal-burning trawlers, experimenting with special insulating chambers to keep fish at freezing point. Ship-repairing was now an important part of the business, and the firm also specialised in lengthening steel vessels. It was at this time too that Alexander's son John started up on his own, establishing his yards across at Torry.

The Duthie's estate at Cairnbulg had meanwhile passed to John Jnr's brother William, the Inches shipbuilder, and subsequently to his son, Sir John Duthie of Cairnbulg, a barrister, a noted Port of London industrialist, a farmer on a grand scale and an opening bat for Aberdeenshire It was he who undertook the restoration of Cairnbulg Castle with the assistance of the Woodside-born artist George R. Gowans, and G. Gordon Jenkins, a founder of the architectural firm of Jenkins & Marr, Aberdeen.

This great shipbuilding and ship-owning dynasty has now passed away. The late Miss Hilda Duthie, almost the last of her line, left Aberdeen Maritime Museum a bequest of £50,000, and thanks to the generosity of the family, the Museum has a number of Duthie artefacts.

Given the way that 'athing hung thegether' in nineteenth century Aberdeen, it is no surprise to learn that George Thompson, principal partner in Walter Hood & Co., the third of the city's great triumvirate of clipper firms, was son-in-law of the famous Dr Kidd of Gilcomston Kirk, whose funeral brought the city to a standstill, and father-in-law of Sir William Henderson of Devanha House, one of the city's most distinguished Lord Provosts. Thompson himself, a radical in politics, was to be Provost of Aberdeen from 1847-49 and its MP from 1852-57. As a lad he had learnt his trade with the Aberdeen-based London Shipping Company, and in 1825 at the age of twenty-one established his own firm, George Thompson & Co., insurance brokers and timber merchants at 38 Marischal Street and launched his first clipper the *Childe Harold* - he had after all been a pupil at Aberdeen Grammar School a few years after Lord Byron. Like many shipowners, he traded with the Baltic, the Mediterranean and North America. He was a truly remarkable man, tall, diginified, kindly and approachable according to Lachlan Mackinnon who was married to his granddaughter. In his *Recollections of an Old Lawyer*, Mackinnon recalled that:

There was a daring and originality in his methods. He told me he had never lost a ship. As the clippers had to carry on in all weathers under press of canvas one must agree that this is a remarkable record. He never insured a ship but built a new one every year with the money saved in premiums. His officers were trained in the service and promoted as they showed merit. When one of them was advanced to a command, his owner made him a present of a 2/64th share of the vessel but on condition that he should not insure the gift, and so would have a personal interest to be careful. The result at least went far to justify the policy.

Walter Hood and Co. had been established in the 1830s. The firm's draughtsman and managing partner, the eponymous Walter Hood, had received his early training at the Fittie yard of J & T Adamson and after pursuing his craft for a time in Dundee, returned to Aberdeen in 1839 to run the new firm that bore his name. A year later, with the first launch anticipated, Hood's were given permission to lay down a patent slip. George Thompson was assumed as principal partner in 1842 and after he took the helm the firm was indeed to build a clipper every year for his White Star Line, taking emigrants Down Under, carrying gold home from the Australian gold rush, or carrying on to China to freight tea, or to Peru for guano.

The 'first generation' of Aberdeen White Star clippers were lauched from Footdee as follows: in 1842, *Neptune* and *Prince of Wales*, in 1846, *Oliver Cromwell* and *Phoenician*. *John Bunyan* followed in 1849 and *Centurion* in 1850 with *Woolloomoolloo* and *Walter Hood* in 1852. *Maid of Judah* was launched

George Thompson, principal partner of Walter Hood & Co and the Aberdeen White Star Line.

in1853, and *Omar Pasha* - one of our allies in the Crimean War, and apparently a household name in Aberdeen - in 1854. *Star of Peace* was built in 1855, *Wave of Life* in 1856. *Damascus* and *Transatlantic* followed in 1857, *Moravian, Strathdon* and *Queen of Nations* in 1858, 1860 and 1861 respectively. That decade also saw the launch of *Kosciusko* in 1862, *Nineveh* and *Ethiopian* in 1864, *George Thompson* in 1865 and *Christiana Thompson* and *Harlaw* in 1866 with *Thyatira* and *Jerusalem* in 1867. *Thermopylae* , the 'pride and wonder of them all was launched in 1868 with *Ascalan* that same year. *Centurion* followed in 1869 and *Aviemore* in 1870.

The earlier of these clippers were designed by Hood at Footdee. *Thermopylae* was designed by Bernard Weymouth, a senior surveyor with Lloyd's Register. Basil Lubbock noted that:

> they were always beautifully kept, easily noticeable amongst other ships for their smartness: indeed when lying in Sydney Harbour with their yards squared to a nicety, their green sides with gilt streak and scroll work at the bow and stern glistening in the sun, their figureheads, masts spars and blocks all painted white and every rope's end flemish coiled on snow white decks, they were the admiration of all who saw them.

Thompson's White Star Line was the first regular trader to Australia. The run was pioneered by the *Phoenician* and *Oliver Cromwell* in 1849, and three years later the *Phoenician* took the record for the quickest passage from Sydney to Plymouth, eighty-three days, with over £81,000 of gold dust aboard, a massive sum in those days. And it was in 1854 that Thompson's son-in-law, the future Sir William Henderson, established the White Star Line's London office. The *Walter Hood, Maid of Judah, Star of Peace* and *Queen of Nations* all made fast passages to Australia, while in 1868, on her maiden voyage under the command of Captain Kemball, the famous *Thermopylae* established the sixty-one day unbeaten record for the London-Melbourne passage under sail. Her best day's run (24 hours) was 380 miles, an achievement that has never been bettered. Only the Clyde-built *Cutty Sark* was her equal, and even here, Footdee can take some kudos. Her designer, Hercules Linton from the Kincardineshire village of Inverbervie, was yet another of Alexander Hall's remarkable apprentices.

Hood himself had died in 1863, and there was an element of black comedy about his passing. Returning from visiting one of his masters whose ship was moored in the Upper Dock, he slipped in the dark and fell between two vessels. The guns of the recently established Torry Battery were fired in the hope that the 'concussion' would bring the body to the surface, but it merely brought folk to their doors. Eventually David Ogilvie, founder of the Torry boat hiring dynasty, was summoned and armed with grappling irons, he eventually succeeded in recovering the corpse. Hood's death, like that of James Hall six years later, cast a gloom over Fittie, for like his friendly rivals, he virtually lived above the shop and was a familiar figure about the place.

Building continued after Hood's death. Clippers for White Star usually filled the stocks, but *Romanoff* in 1874 and *Cimba* in 1878 were purpose-built

The Cimba, built by Hood for Alexander Nicol & Sons.

for Alexander Nicol & Son's Australian wool trade. *Romanoff* had an inauspicious start on her initial run to London. She battled against a contrary wind from the start, and after ten days, was no further south than Stonehaven. Worse still, she had run out of liquid refreshment of the type favoured by seafarers and had to hail a passing vessel for fresh supplies, and was accordingly dubbed 'Rumenough'.

A chapter noting briefly the clippers launched at the Footdee yards is not really the place to recall their numerous adventures, but an exception can be made for the *Cimba*, (Swahili for lion), one of Hood's most beautiful vessels, a tender ship, it was said, requiring a master hand. She was involved in a fearful row on completing her maiden voyage to Sydney harbour. Her master, Captain Fimister, jumped the queue into *Patriarch*'s loading berth and refused to move back to his proper place. Complaints were made to the Colonial Secretary and when the harbourmaster tried to board, Fimister threatened to throw him overboard. He was eventually fined, but the episode was the talk of Sydney, and one wonders what the owner, Lord Provost Nicol must have thought of it all when he learnt the news.

From the late 1860s, Walter Hood was busily involved in constructing a 'second generation' of wool clippers for the Aberdeen White Star Line, iron built, larger than their predecessors and forsaking the Aberdeen Bow to give them more cargo space. *Patriarch*, the first, launched in 1869, held the Sydney to London record of 68 days. She was followed by *Militades* in 1871, who in common with many of her successors had a name drawn from Greek history, though not, of course, the *Samuel Plimsoll*, built in 1873 and named after the renowned Member of Parliament whose campaign for greater safety and improved conditions at sea was making him unpopular with many shipowners at that time. White Star, as noted, had a record for safety second to none and Plimsoll declared himself much honoured when invited to Footdee to launch the very fast, beautiful, clipper that bore his name.

Salamis followed in 1875, and then came *Aristides*, in 1876, the White Star flagship, initially under the command of Captain Kemball, and at 1661 tons the largest Hood clipper. *Smyrna* was launched in the same year and *Pericles* in 1877. She was launched at Footdee on the same tide as Duthie's *Brilliant* and the two clippers enjoyed great rivalry on the Sydney run. The pretty *Sophocles* followed in 1879 and was thought still to be trading after the First World War. *Orontes* was Hood's last clipper, launched in 1881, the year the firm merged with Alexander Hall & Co. By the late 1870s the triple expansion engine, with its higher steam pressure and reduced fuel consumption was being successfully adopted to merchant ships. The day of the clipper was drawing to a close, and the Footdee yards were turning now to the production of screw streamers. The second *Thermopylae*, built by Hall Russell for the White Star Line in 1891, though still with elegant lines, was a steamship.

The Samuel Plimsoll, built by Walter Hood & Co for the White Star Line.

Captain Thomas Wyness, Harbour Master at Aberdeen from 1922 to 1939 served with the line from 1887 until 1892 and sailed in a number of those later clippers, retaining vivid memories of them all. In the early 1890s he was apprentice on the *Aristides* , 'one of the finest and fastest of her kind.' She was laden with wool and running east towards Cape Horn when they drew abreast with a Liverpool steamer, carrying mails and passengers to New Zealand:

> I can see as if it were yesterday our master, Captain Nathan Allan, hanging on with his left hand to the weather mizzen shrouds, intent on passing the steamer. All hands remained on deck to see the show and bear a hand if need be. Sure enough in the middle of the dog watch we were abreast of her and could see her passengers waving to us and our good ship....They would never see the like again - a race between a full-rigged clipper and a mail steamer with Wind beating Steam hollow.

The *Aristides* overtook the steamer, crossed her bow 'and got to the windward of her which is a daring thing to do at sea, and nothing less than a piece of impertinence from a sailing ship to a mail steamer'. And Captain Wyness concluded his yarn in an elegiac style:

> As you might suppose, all hands were called aft for grog. But before midnight the wind fell away and the steamer gradually overhauled and passed us. And so it proved in the end for all sailing ships. The steamers gradually overhauled and passed them and at last drove them from the sea. And no one regrets it more than the few surviving sailors who sailed the seas in the beautiful sailing clippers of the Aberdeen Line.

Advertisements used by Hall and Hall Russell in their heyday.

Chapter 15

Hall Russell

Hall Russell....a household name in Aberdeen.
Press and Journal, April 11, 1986.

The Footdee shipbuilding firm of Hall Russell & Co., for so long a household word in Aberdeen, was set up in September 1864, but was its creation really necessary? Of the four founding partners, James and William Hall had headed Alexander Hall & Co., Aberdeen's largest shipbuilding firm, renowned for its record-breaking vessels, since their father's retirement in 1835. They were not adverse to the new technology for they had been building hulls for steam-driven vessels since 1840. If they felt they were were getting too old - James was sixty and William fifty-seven - to make a wholehearted transition to iron ships and steam-engines as other firms were doing, why not involve the next Hall generation? William's own sons, and the son of their sister Ann Wilson, had all trained as shipwrights at the family yard. Surely they were eager to prove themselves masters of the new technology. And during this transition period, why not seek out a manager experienced in steam from among their numerous contacts in the trade. Indeed the Glasgow engineer, Thomas Russell, appointed managing partner of the new firm at an annual salary of £550 was just such a man. Why not have invited him to join the management of Halls instead?

The clue for the creation of Hall Russell lies in the date. As we saw in Chapter 13, George Thomson of the rope-making firm Catto & Thomson had 'absconded' as William put it, in 1863, leaving the Halls struggling to pay a debt of £25,000, with worse to follow. A new company would, on the other hand, commence with a clean sheet and be financially better placed to invest in modern technology than the debt-ridden Alexander Hall & Co. Moreover J C Couper, the fourth founding partner of Hall Russell, had valuable contracts in the Orient. One imagines that he would not relish doing deals on behalf of a firm that was on the brink of financial disaster.

John Couper, an old China hand if so formidable a personality can be thus described had been another of Halls' remarkable apprentices. Having served his time as a shipwright, he set off for China where he made his fortune, establishing shipyards at Whampoa near Canton, and in Hong Kong where the district became known as Aberdeen Harbour. He returned to Britain in 1863 and settled initially in the south of England.

Thomas Russell, managing partner at Hall Russell.

The contract of copartnery shows that the initial capital of £20,000 was, on paper at least, contributed equally by the four partners, and the opportunity was taken to provide the Halls with some ready cash. From the initial capital, £14,000 was immediately handed over to the brothers in return for making available to Hall Russell various Catto assets including 'ground, machinery, houses and other buildings at Footdee'.

It is usually assumed that Hall Russell was set up initially to make boilers and ships' engines. This was not the case. William Simpson's former York Place Iron Works had been acquired and modernised as its headquarters, but the firm was nevertheless founded as Hall Russell & Co., Iron Shipbuilders, Aberdeen, and was straightway given the use of Halls' 'upper yard to build iron ships'. Couper, writing from Surrey with advice on suitable courses of action to follow, emerges as the firm's *éminence grise*. The minutes of 20 April 1865 record: 'Took into consideration a letter from J C Couper dated 27th March relative to Gun Boats - resolved to tender for them at £15,000'. It is interesting to note that James Milne, managing director of Hall Russell from 1980-85, used to say: 'We quote for anything that floats,' but this was the watchword from the very start. The firm went after everything from gunboats to tugboats and Halls and Hall Russell lived in each others pockets. In March 1865, for example, Hall Russell tendered to build a steamer at £21,000. This was undertaken as a joint venture with Alexander Hall & Co. building the hull for £12,000 while Hall Russell provided the engines and boilers for £9000. This

Hall Russel's first ship, the Kwang Tung, was a joint venture with Alexander Hall & Co. Note the fine view of Waterloo Quay including the Aberdeen Steam Office, extreme right.

explains why the *Kwang Tung* for Douglas Lapraik & Co. of Hong Kong, a Couper contact, appears both on Halls' and Hall Russell's list, indeed as the latter's first iron ship in 1868. John Couper was back in Aberdeen by the end of 1865 and soon after bought the estate of Craigiebuckler when its owner, a scion of the Blaikie family, also absconded with massive debts - but that is another story. Couper, now 'of Craigiebuckler', took the chair at partners' meetings, held either in the York Place Iron Works or at Waterside, and appeared to be in charge in those early days, making the name of Hall Russell something of a misnomer!

As noted in Chapter 13 relations between the Hall brothers were strained after 1867 when their nephew, A Hall Wilson, James'protégé, was assumed as a partner in Hall Russell with the gift of half James' share. The Minutes call for 'mutual forbearance' and 'good feeling'. And although the brothers had an understandable contretemps at a difficult time, relations with the workforce were, on the whole, to be good throughout the firm's history. On Hogmanay 1868, the partners not only 'coutenanced' a 'Social Meeting of the Workmen at the Music Hall', but financed it as well.

The Hall brothers' connection with Hall Russell ended in 1869, their saddest year, when James's sudden death was followed by the insolvency of Alexander Hall & Co. William assigned his shares to Couper who continued in partnership with Russell and A Hall Wilson. Couper and Russell retired in 1877 and two years later Hall Russell became a limited liability company. Two Aberdonians, John Scott and James Hunter who had been asssumed as partners in 1874 now continued at the helm with A Hall Wilson.

Rapid growth followed. The firm was one of the pioneers of the triple expansion engine whose ecomonic use of fuel had at last made the steamship viable and customers in the 1880s included the Indo-China Steam Navigation Co., Chinese and Indian steamship companies and at home, the North of Scotland Orkney and Shetland Steam Navigation Co. Indeed, one of Hall Russell's last contracts a hundred years later was for the *St Sunniva* for North of Scotland's successor, P & O Ferries. Between 1869 and 1910 the firm built a fleet of graceful passenger and cargo steamers, the 'In' vessels, for John T Rennie's Aberdeen Line which traded between London and South Africa. These included the *Induna* (1891), the *Inanda* (1904) and the splendidly fitted out *Intaba* (1910), at that time the largest steamer built in Footdee. Apart from bringing in the steel, which was replacing iron by the 1880s, Hall Russell was entirely self-sufficient, and the firm's craftmanship a byword in the industry. The short-lived *Thermopylae* built in 1891 for the Aberdeen White Star Line (not to be confused with Hood's record-breaking clipper of 1868) had acccommodation for fifty first class and 300 third class passengers complete with music rooms, dining saloon and state rooms, and the vessel 'was fitted up with electricity - quite a new development'. Hall Russell long had a reputation not only for employing generations of riveters, platers, boilermakers and caulkers who handed down their skills to sons and nephews, but cabinetmakers and French polishers as well, many of whose time-sheets have been meticulously preserved. Photographs of the ferry, the *Earl Thorfinn* for example, reveal handsome balustrades, fine woodwork and plush upholstery in the first class saloon.

The acquisition of John Duthie Sons & Co. in 1907 allowed access to the harbour and a foothold in York Street. By the outbreak of the First World War, Hall Russell's yard occupied five acres to the west of Halls' and the firm, employing 1400 men, was equipped with the latest technology including gas-fired furnaces and an overhead travelling crane. As with Halls, trawlers had been the firm's major output since 1884. Between 1891 and 1930, over sixty 'Strath' trawlers for John Brown of Redhall's Aberdeen Steam Trawling and Fishing Co. Ltd. went down the slips, sometimes in tandem. Many were requisitioned for minesweeping during the 1914-18 War including the *Strathlochy* launched in 1916 which became the prototype for around 150 Admiralty Strath-class minesweeping trawlers. In a touching gesture these vessels were named after the ships' companies of *Victory* and *Royal Sovereign* which had fought at Trafalgar. Of these Hall Russell built the *William Barlow*, the *John Braskett* and many more.

The York Place Iron Works, later Hall Russell's Engine Shop.

Colliers launched for local coal merchants included three *Sprays* between 1887 and 1962 for Ellis & McHardy, two *Thrifts* in 1904 and 1931 for the Northern Co-op, the second *Redhall* which was at Dunkirk, and two *Ferryhills* in 1909 and 1919 for the Aberdeen Coal Company. These unglamorous vessels were local favourites, particularly the second *Thrift* which berthed in the Upper Dock. In the summer of 1947, the *Christian Radich*, a handsome Norwegian sail training ship, leaving on the tide after a courtesy visit, her cadets manning the yards, was preceded by the grimy *Thrift* which got as loud a cheer as the elegant Norwegian, rather to her crew's embarrassment.

Tragedy had struck early in the Second World War. On 12 July, 1940, a Heinkel whose projected target was RAF Leuchars, jettisoned a stick of bombs over the city while attempting to escape from pursuing Spitfires. Hall Russell took an inadvertent direct hit which left thirty-two dead and 100 injured. Those who had gathered in the boiler shop near the main entrance for their dinner break were trapped, and the engine shop in the old York Place Iron Works, was also badly damaged. It was cruelly ironic for the premises should have been closed for the Trades Week but the war effort demanded that production go ahead. The York Place frontage of Hall Russell and the engine shop in the former Iron Works took the full brunt of the bomb and bore the scars, visible in the patched-in concrete at the base of their walls. The Hall

View from the main gate. The former boiler shop to the left, the 'Empire Exhibition' building right.

Russell frontage was demolished in 1993, but the concrete repairs are still visible at the old Iron Works

During the war Hall Russell built Bay and River class frigates, Flower class corvettes, and landing craft of various designs for the Royal Navy. James Fraser, former chief ships' draughtsman who joined the firm in 1939 and spent his whole career there as so many did, still recalls how prefabricated sections of these warships, delivered by lady drivers, were stored on the Links owing to lack of space in the yard.

The end of a long family association had come in 1942 when Hall Russell was acquired by the Burntisland Shipping Co. Ltd., and the chairman, A Hall Wilson Jnr, a great grandson of Alexander Hall and the fifth generation from James Cochar retired at that time. Jock Smith, formerly head foreman loftsman, who had started his shipwright's apprenticeship in 1940, remembers him as one of the old school, bowler-hatted and chauffeur-driven. The takeover, which brought in Howard Johnson as managing director was regarded as good for Hall Russell, for Burnistland was a modern firm with progressive ideas. Friendship grew between the two yards, Jock Smith recalls, and they enjoyed a joint annual sports day.

After the war the Footdee premises were modernised. The familiar building that lay straight ahead from the main gate was erected at this time to house the electrical and carpenters' shops as well as offices and stores. It had been purchased at the Empire Exhibibition of 1939 and brought north, but lay in storage during the war owing to the unavailability of steel required for its erection. The place now went like a fair, the workforce striving to replace the mercantile and fishing fleets lost through enemy action. Staff were both proud and amazed to find Hall Russell trawlers of the 1890s coming in for refit. The little shops nearby prospered and apprentices and office boys would queue at the 'Co-opie' baker in St Clement Street with orders for break-time baps and rowies.

In 1947, Scotland's first motor trawler, the *Star of Scotland* left the stocks at Pocra, the beginning of the end for the coal-burning era. The *Sir William Hardy* followed in 1955, destined for experimental work at the Torry Research Station. The prototype for the modernisation of the British trawler fleet, she was the first diesel electric all-refrigerated trawler to be built in the UK. Seagoing scientists experimented with advanced techniques of catch-handling and processing in her custom-built laboratories. After twenty-two years service this sturdy vessel was decommissioned, then purchased by the Greenpeace organisation. She now enjoyed a second, hectic career in defence of the environment as *Rainbow Warrior,* meeting her fate eventually in 1985 in Auckland Harbour when she was blown up by the French Secret Service.

Hall Russell absorbed Halls during the 1950s as already noted, and now occupied twelve acres in the York Place, York Street and Pocra Quay areas - indeed the entire original fishers' haven of Pockraw - leased in almost equal portions from Aberdeen Town Council and Aberdeen Harbour Board. Among the more surprising of the assets which came to Hall Russell at this time were two elderly but sturdy handcarts, dating back probably to the days of sail, and useful amid all the 'high tech' equipment, for trundling heavy items across the cassies of York Place. The workforce still numbered close to a thousand in those days and George Webster recalls on occasions being caught up with the men leaving the yard whilst he was cycling back home to the Squares. He would be swept down St Clement Street, bicycle and all, by the sheer force of numbers. A queue of double-decker buses awaited those who lived further afield. Many workers, however,lived in the area including Neptune Terrace and York Street, and Hall Russell was quite often landlord as well as employer.

Numerous challenges were met by John Wright who became managing director in 1955 and chairman in 1968. A wide range of specialised vessels were constructed during this era; bulk carriers for raw sugar and molasses; prototype freezer trawlers; passenger and cargo vessels for Canada; coastal tankers; deep sea trawlers for South Africa; collier fleets for English Gas and Electricity Boards; ocean going yachts; fast liners with sophisticated cargo-handling devices for the German, French and Dutch governments, the last placing a contract for the *Thameshaven* which at 10,500 tons, was the largest

181

to be built in Aberdeen and protruded into York Street; a £500,000 oil rig supply ship, the *Lady Alison* for P & O, the first to be built by a British yard.

Hall Russell had survived the collapse of Burntisland Shipping in 1968 and was now owned by Northern Shipbuilding and Industrial Holdings Ltd. When orders began to run low, John Wright took the gamble of building a versatile offshore supply vessel in 1973, designed to cope with northern north sea conditions, with powerful towing capacity and a bowthruster capable of operating in any direction which made her highly manoeuvrable. His decision to build 'on spec' was also aimed both at keeping the workforce together and alerting the government as to the difficulties experienced by British firms in competing against heavily subsidised foreign rivals. The £1 million vessel, *Lady Sylvia*, was eventually purchased by a P & O subsidiary. This episode occasioned an unsolicited panegyric from Peter Emery, then Head of the Department of Trade and Industry on John Wright's effort on behalf of British industry. An order for two supply vessels followed from the giant Tidewater Marine Services Inc. of Louisiana, operators of the largest supply fleet in the world, though the deal was done on a fixed price basis, the bane of all shipbuilders. By mid-1974, Hall Russell had seven or eight ships on hand and the order book was full for eighteen months ahead. The engine shop based at the old York Street Iron Works was fitted out to undertake the specialised repairing of offshore installations and a new dry dock capable of taking vessels up to 370ft was in operation. One demanding order that year was a car-passenger ferry built to exacting specifications for the Scrabster- Stromness run which Hall Russell successfully secured against bids from seven British and foreign yards.

Multi-million pound Ministry of Defence orders in the 1970s and 1980s included Island class patrol vessels such as *HMS Jersey*, followed during 1980-82 by three markedly more powerful Castle class 'mini-warships' designed to protect offshore gas and oil installations as well as the traditional fishing grounds. And during 1983 and 1984, five Peacock class gunboats slipped away from Pocra in the dawn, destined to patrol Hong Kong waters. While the earlier Ministry of Defence craft carried Bofors guns, *Swift*, *Starling* and the other Peacock class ships were fitted out with Italian weaponry worth several million pounds. Their role included the interception of illegal immigrants attempting to enter Hong Kong from China. In 1985, three mooring and salvage ships used for retrieving wrecks were commissioned by the Ministry of Defence.

Douglas Paul succeeded John Wright as managing director, and Jock Smith has many memories of the personalities of those days; the yard manager George Milne, Colin MacLeay, the general manager popularly known as 'The Bud', and the portly pipe-smoking John Clausen, foreman plater, one of the old school. And it fell to James Milne, who had entered the drawing office as

HMS Peacock, right, one of the gunboats destined for Hong Kong, fitting out at Hall Russell. In the foreground HMS Plover has just been launched.

a lad in 1939, and become managing director in 1980, and to his successor Joe Craig, to preside over the last rites of Hall Russell.

The firm had been nationalised in 1977. Seven years earlier, demarcation had been abolished and the workforce given a broad training with the result that in spite of fluctuations within the industry, jobs were saved and there were no major strikes. Regarded as 'the jewel in the crown' of British Shipbuilders, Hall Russell, unlike the latter's other components, consistently returned a profit, and consequently, with a change in government was regarded as ideal for privatisation. Hall Russell was put on the market in July 1984, and there was much apprehension in Aberdeen that the yard might be acquired for rig repair or pipeline storage. The entire workforce, the people of Aberdeen, the Church, local authorities and the press campaigned vigorously for a government guarantee that a shipbuilding facility would be retained at Footdee.

In spite of Hall Russell's fine record, three 'buyout' plans proved abortive. The first, a management-workforce plan in tandem with Yarrow's failed when the Clydesiders voted against it and the bankers withdrew. But the main reason behind the failure of these proposals was the anomalous, even farcical situation in which Hall Russell was placed. Although not a traditional naval yard, the EC had classed it as such, rendering the firm ineligible to apply for a 28 per cent subsidy from the EC intervention fund for merchant class work, and thus unable to compete on equal terms for such work. The situation was compounded when, in 1985, the Ministry of Defence announced that no further naval work, on which the yard had set such store, would be forthcoming. The other potential bidders, the Sproat-Belch consortium - Ross Belch was a Clydeside shipbuilder of repute - and British Aerospace, quite naturally lost interest. It is no exaggeration to say that there was a feeling of bitterness and betrayal abroad in Aberdeen at that time.

In 1986 Hall Russell was eventually acquired by a local consortium, Aberdeen Shipbuilders Ltd., who had high hopes of retaining the warship building capacity of the now privatised firm, while pursuing orders for specialist offshore vessels, restructuring the company, offering long term employment and refitting the work-

James Milne, managing director, 1980 - 85

shops with 'state of the art' technology. Apart from some repair and maintenance work, however, the only major order forthcoming was in 1987 for a ferry destined for the South Atlantic dependencies of St Helena and Ascension Island, and that was secured only after intense lobbying. Funding to the tune of £19 million was provided by the Overseas Development Agency. However

The shop stewards who led the campaign to retain Hall Russell for shipbuilding in 1984

in November 1988, before the *St Helena* was completed, Aberdeen Shipbuilders went into liquidation. Jock Smith, as it happened, retired the following day. His first ship as a sixteen-year-old-apprentice had been a French prison ship, *Bois Rose*, and now *St Helena* was to be his, and Hall Russell's last. The following year it was revealed that the firm had gone down with debts of some £10 milllion.

The name of Hall Russell vanished forever in February 1989 when the yard was acquired by A & P Appledore of Tyneside, owned by Peter de Savary, and run as one of its subsidiaries. The *St Helena* was eventually launched by the new firm in October 1989. In December 1991, however, Appledore threw in the towel after a joint venture with a Dutch firm, Volker Stevin, failed to find offshore repair work. Aberdeen Ship Repair, a Clydeside subsidiary, was lauched the following month and leased part of the yard with the aim of tendering for repair work, but it too folded less than a year later.

There was a day of much sadness in May 1993 when what had once been Hall Russell plant and equipment was auctioned off at the yard, much of it according to old timers, going for a fraction of the original cost. By that time, virtually the whole of the Hall Russell yard - formal communications apart, I don't think it was ever referred to as A & P Appledore - had vanished. Aberdeen Harbour Board was in the throes of converting the site into a multi-berth facility to provide much needed space for port users. Four deep water

The firm's last ship, the St Helena was completed by A&P Appledore in 1989.
Courtesy, Alex Guyan.

berths were created to accommodate the largest of the offshore support vessels, so the old haven of Pockraw has in a sense, reverted to one of its earlier roles. That latter day landmark, the massive covered construction hall, which Hall Russell had brought up from Clydeside and erected in 1982, was truncated for Harbour Board use with the demounted section reinstated as a transit shed. Older industrial buildings have been demolished, but the dry dock was retained and leased in 1993 to the George Craig Group, a local company with numerous harbour and offshore interests. Thus the skill of ship repairing continues at Footdee. The slipway of 1869 has been preserved as an item of historical importance and the former York Place Iron Works soldiers on, leased at time of writing to a mud firm. The Hall Russell Training Centre, set up in 1968 in the old Alexander Hall & Co offices in York Street to train apprentice shipbuilders, was bought out by its management, headed by the director, James Shearer. It now continues as the Industrial Training Centre, Aberdeen, training young people in a range of skills including marine engineering, fabrication, welding, joinery and electrical and clerical work. But there are no shipbuilding apprentices anymore.

The name of Hall Russell has all but vanished. The prize winning Hall Russell Male Voice Choir whose membership extended beyond the yard is long gone and the Hall Russell Social and Recreation Club closed in 1992, its membership dwindling. Today the name is alone retained by the Hall Russell Junior football team.

Courtesy, Alex Guyan

Postscript 1997

Since 1993 there have been a number of changes in the Fittie area. Garvock Wynd, which once led from the Links to the Shorelands, and latterly from Links Place to Miller Street has been blocked off from the Links end, while Church Street and Miller Street have been tarmacadamed and the engine rails lifted (page 123). In St Clement Street, the sturdy Co-op tenement next to the churchyard (page 129) has been replaced by blue and white industrial units which extend round the back of the St Clements Bar from what used to be Links Street.

The gable-end of the former Gourock Ropeworks, earlier still, Duthies - all that remains of St Clement Place - and now incorporated into the premises of Strachans Ltd, has been attractively refurbished by that firm. Beyond is a new unit occupied by G McWilliam Ltd, catering butchers, again in blue and white.

The gable-end of the former Gourock Ropeworks, now part of Strachan's Ltd has been attractively refurbished.

This was the site of the Hall Russell furnace, where locals could have a warm against the stone wall which was always hot. Opposite, John Smith's fine building (page 33) requires restoration. Hall Russell of course is gone, its quayside given over to deep water berths. Of the five Peacock patrol vessels built there to serve in Hong Kong waters, (page182), *Swift* and *Swallow*, now *Orla* and *Ciara* were bought by the Irish Republic in 1988; *Peacock*, *Plover* and *Starling* were sold to the Philippines and left Hong Kong for Manila at midnight on 30 June 1997 when the colony reverted to China. Thus was Hall Russell's last link with the Far East severed.

The new McWilliam unit contrasts starkly with the industrial architecture of the former Hall Russell engineering shed beyond, where that firm had its beginnings.

In York Street, Halls' former sheds and the Hall Russell canteen have been demolished (page 131). Between the Neptune Bar and the bus shelter, (now restored!) are Seaforth Maritime, who have abandoned their Waterloo Quay offices for the Mobil North Sea Oil site, R & M Engineering and Dales Marine Services. York Street Nursery School, (page 62) was closed down by the local authority after a proud history, and the premises put on the market in 1997. In that same year a new system was at last installed to carry sewage to the outfall at Nigg (page 115), bringing with it fears for the future of Scarty's Monument, the old ventilator shaft, a familiar Fittie landmark.

The Squares themselves remain clean, attractive, well kept and blissfully traffic free.

HMS Starling, ex-Hall Russell, heading for Hong Kong with an escort of six Fast Pursuit Craft (FPC) manned by Royal Marines. Courtesy, British Forces, Hong Kong.

Select Bibliography

Books

Anson, Peter, *Fishing Boats and Fisher Folk*, J M Dent, 1930

Brogden, W A, *Aberdeen, An Ilustrated Architectural Guide*, RIAS, 1986

Clark, Victoria, *The Port of Aberdeen*, D Wyllie & Son, 1922

Douglas, Francis, *A General Description of the East Coast of Scotland*, Paisley, 1782

Fraser, G M *Historical Aberdeen*, The Bon-Accord Press, 1905

Gammie, Alexander, *The Churches of Aberdeen*, Aberdeen Daily Journal, 1909

Kennedy, William, *Annals of Aberdeen*, 2 Vols, London, 1818

Lubbock, Basil, *The Colonial Clippers*, Brown, Son & Ferguson, 1948

Mackinnon, Lachlan, *Recollections of an Old Lawyer*, D Wyllie & Son, 1935

Perren, Richard, *John Fleming & Comany Limited* 1877-1977, privately published

Reid, John S. *Mechanical Aberdeen*, KMP/JSR, 1990

Robertson, Joseph, *The Book of Bon Accord*, Lewis Smith, 1839

Skene, William, *East Neuk Chronicles*, Aberdeen Daily Journal, 1905

Spalding, John, *Memorialls of the Trubles in Scotland and in England*, Spalding Club, 1850

Turner, John R, *Scotland's North Sea Gateway*, AUP 1986

Booklets, Pamphlets, Articles

Allardyce, Ann, 'Footdee in the Eighteenth Century', *The Goodwife at Home*, Bon-Accord Booklets, 1867

Allen, Greg, 'Our Silver Penny', *Leopard Magazine*, November 1982 - February 1983

Baxter, Andrew, *Bygone Days of Footdee*, Typescript, nd

Baxter, Rosemary, *St Clement's Parish, Aberdeen*, Aberdeen & North-East Scotland Family History Society, 1989

Brown, Jimmy, 'Little But Good: The Great North of Scotland Railway', *Leopard Magazine*, May, 1978

Carnegie, Hazel, *Harnessing the Wind*, Centre for Scottish Studies, Aberdeen University

McKay, Alexander, 'Modern Japan', *Leopard Magazine*, March, 1989

Morgan, Diane, 'John Wright of Hall Russell', *Business Scotland*, February, 1974

Mulford Susan Fettes, 'Seaforth Maritime: the first ten years', *Leopard Magazine*, June, 1982

Myers, Peter, 'Coals to Aberdeen', *Leopard Magazine*, March-April, 1980

Spiers, Sheila , *The Kirkyard of St Clement's (Aberdeen)*, Aberdeen & North-East Scotland Family History Society, 1988

Waterman J J, *Aberdeen and the Fishing Industry in the 1870s*, Centre for Scottish Studies, Aberdeen University

Manuscripts

Aberdeen City Archives: Council Registers Vols LXVIII - XCV, Lists of Alexander Hall & Co. Ltd. and Hall Russell & Co Ltd., Hall Russell & Co. Minute Book 1865-1879, miscellaneous documents relating to Aberdeen Harbour and Footdee.

Aberdeen City Libraries: The Aberdeen Footdee Society Minute Book, 1761 - 1820

Grampian Regional Archives: Logs and Admission Registers of Commerce Street, Frederick Street, Hanover Street, St Clement Street and York Street Schools

Index